THE
CATACOMBS

Life and Death in
Early Christianity

THE CATACOMBS

Life and Death in Early Christianity

James Stevenson

Thomas Nelson Publishers
Nashville • Camden • New York

Copyright © 1978 by Thames and Hudson Ltd., London

Published in the United States by Thomas Nelson, Inc., Nashville, Tennessee, and distributed in Canada by Lawson Falle Ltd., Cambridge, Ontario. First American printing in paperback: 1985.

LIBRARY OF CONGRESS CATALOGING
IN PUBLICATION DATA

Stevenson, James, 1901-1983
  The catacombs : life and death in early Christianity.

  Originally published: London : Thames and Hudson,
1978.
  Bibliography: p.
  Includes index.
  1. Catacombs—Italy—Rome. 2. Catacombs.
3. Christian antiquities—Italy—Rome. 4. Christian
antiquities. 5.Church history—Primitive and early
church, ca. 30-600. 6. Rome (Italy)—Antiquities.
7. Italy—Antiquities. I. Title.
DG807.4.S74 1985   270;.1   85-341
ISBN 0-807-7500-8 (pbk.)

Contents

Acknowledgments

I have been helped by various individuals in the preparation of this book, and I take this opportunity of thanking them. Some of them may have forgotten the occasions on which they helped me, but I have not. Any statements made in the book, and any errors are mine alone. The fault is likewise mine if I have omitted anyone from the following list: S.-L. Agnello, A. Bertucci, M. H. Braüde, A. L. Davies, U. Fasola, G. Ferrari, A. Ferrua, J. Galea, O. Garana, J. Gray, T. J. Harrington, Janet Huskinson, F. Mallia, T. Molony, P. Testini, G. Theureu, J. B. Ward Perkins, M. A. Waters, C. G. Zammit. My thanks are also due to various *fossores* and members of the staff at catacombs for guidance on long walks in the darkness.

1

The Making of the Catacombs

Quel travail, en effet, pour creuser les innombrables galeries des catacombes romaines.

A. F. Leynaud, *Les catacombes africaines*

On the Via Appia Antica, about two miles from the Aurelian walls of Rome, there is a locality that became known in antiquity as *ad* or *in Catacumbas*. From the second half of the third century AD a centre of Christian veneration of the Apostles Peter and Paul existed here and, from the fourth century, a Christian underground burial place. From this site, though in fact it was not the earliest of its type, the name 'catacomb' has spread to other underground cemeteries in widely separated countries. The most notable catacombs are those in the immediate vicinity of Rome, but important ones are to be found at Naples, at Syracuse and other places in Sicily, in Malta and in North Africa, and in the East at Emesa in Syria.

In meaning, the word 'catacomb' has nothing to do with burial places. The early Christians called these *coemeteria* – places of repose – and this name persisted among them, being particularly used of burial places above ground. The Latin expression *ad Catacumbas* conceals a Greek original, *kata kumbas*, which means something like 'at the hollows'. Such a meaning is not unsuitable to the topography of the area, as the ground slopes steeply to a declivity which the Via Appia crosses, and beyond which, as one looks away from the city, the prominent tomb of Caecilia Metella can be seen on rising ground. The two Greek words became regarded as one Latin word, to which the preposition *ad* or *in* (at) was prefixed. This was the only underground cemetery near Rome that was visited during all succeeding centuries.

The early Christians, like their pagan contemporaries, regarded the burial of the dead as a duty of supreme importance, particularly when individuals belonged to the same household or

7

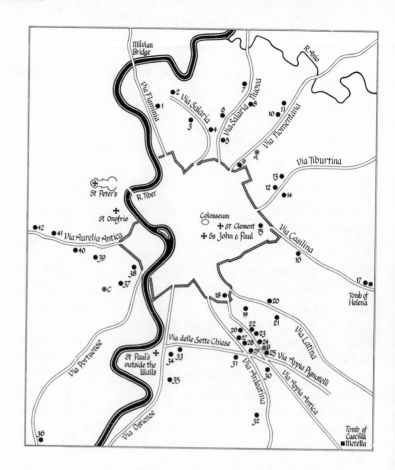

1 Rome and the catacombs in its vicinity

KEY

1 Valentine

2 'Ad Clivum Cucumeris' [?]

3 Bassilla (Hermes)

4 Pamphilus

5 Felicity

6 Thrason

7 Priscilla

8 Jordani

9 Nicomedes

10 Agnes

11 *Coemeterium Maius*

12 Novatian

13 Hippolytus

14 Cyriaca (St Laurence)

15 Hypogaeum of the Aurelii

16 Castulus

17 Peter and Marcellinus

18 Campana

19 Gordian and Epimachus

20 Apronian

21 Via Dino Campagni (Via Latina)

22 Vibia

23 The Hunters

24 The Cross (Sta Croce)

25 Praetextatus

26 Soter

27 Balbina

28 Basileus (Marcus and Marcellianus)

29 Callistus (incl. Lucina)

30 'Ad Catacumbas' (St Sebastian)

31 Domitilla

32 Nunziatella

33 Commodilla

34 Timothy

35 Thecla

36 Generosa

37 Pontian

38 'Ad Insalsatos' [?]

39 Pancras

40 Processus and Martinian

41 'Duo Felices'

42 Calepodius

Jewish Catacombs

A Villa Torlonia

B Vigna Randanini

C Monte Verde

association (*societas*). In AD 251, in the worst days of the persecution under Decius, the clergy of Rome, bereft of a bishop through the martyrdom of Fabian, wrote to the clergy of Carthage, also bereft of a bishop through the retirement of Cyprian from that city. They did not approve of Cyprian's conduct, and took it on themselves to remind their Carthaginian colleagues of various duties. 'The greatest of these is', they write, 'that, if the bodies of martyrs and others are not buried, a great responsibility lies on those whose duty this is. So any of you who has carried out this work on any occasion is, we are sure, judged by God as the good servant who, faithful in the least things, will be made ruler over ten cities.' But even fifty years before this the Christian community was taking a corporate interest in burials. In Tertullian's *Apology* (*c.* 197) we are told that the collections made monthly were used among other things to feed and to bury the poor, and in his *De Anima* a Presbyter prays at the funeral of a Christian woman, for the peace of her soul. Later, towards the end of the fourth century, Ambrose declared that in order to secure proper burial for Christians, it was permitted to break up, melt and sell even the sacred vessels of the Church.

A half century later than Cyprian, Lactantius, in his work on *The Principles of True Religion*, laid down the forms that Christian action should take. Among the duties involved was that of burial not only of friends and relatives, but also of the poor and strangers. Like Cyprian's Roman correspondents, he calls this the greatest of duties, and contrasts the Christian attitude with that of the pagans, among whom the poor and unwanted might be thrust into horrible *puticoli*, pits for promiscuous burial. There was of course also a theological reason for Christian care of the dead, i.e. the firm belief in a bodily resurrection, a theme to be elaborated by Prudentius towards the end of the fourth century in his burial hymn (*Cathemerinon* XI). As the pagan Caecilius says in his anti-Christian speech in the *Octavius* of Minucius Felix (*c.* AD 220), 'they [the Christians] curse our funeral pyres and condemn cremation', and he goes on to scoff at the Christians' eschatological expectations.

'Devout men buried Stephen', says the Acts of the Apostles of the first martyr, and from that time onwards they recovered bodies of martyrs, where possible; such recovery was allowed by Roman law, though ill-disposed persons tried to prevent this, e.g. in the case of Polycarp at Smyrna in AD 156. The pagans well knew this Christian preoccupation, and, for example at Lyons in

AD 177, took steps to counter it by burning the bodies of the martyrs, and throwing the ashes into the River Rhône. Similarly in AD 303 the bodies of imperial servants who were martyrs were exhumed and thrown into the sea 'lest any, regarding them as actually gods, should worship them as they lay in their tombs'.[1] Later still, at Alexandria in 361, when George, the city's intruding bishop and others were lynched by a mob, the populace burnt their bodies and flung the ashes into the sea, lest a martyr-shrine should be raised over them. Ignatius of Antioch, on his way to martyrdom in Rome about AD 115 expresses the hope that his body may be destroyed by the beasts, so that he would not be a trouble to anyone. Finally, the apostate emperor Julian, in 362, in his efforts to reform paganism, mentioned various reasons for the success and popularity of Christianity. Among these is 'their care for the graves of the dead'.

Initially, when Christians were few, the duty of sepulture must have been carried out by individuals, or by their servants, in the cemeteries used by the pagans, as was done in the case of St Peter and St Paul. Polycarp at Smyrna, about AD 156, and Justin and his companions at Rome about AD 165 were laid 'where it was fitting', or 'in a convenient place'. We may be sure that such burials took place in pagan cemeteries though we find that Cyprian blamed a lapsed Spanish bishop for belonging to a pagan burial club and allowing the funeral rites of members of his family to take place in such surroundings. Later on, in the fourth century, Hilary of Poitiers and the Council of Laodicea could warn Christians against burial with the pagans, and the frequenting of pagan cemeteries, but in earlier times such a prohibition was hardly possible, and we shall see examples of pagan and Christian burial side by side. When Christian cemeteries began to be constructed, for example round Rome, on the properties of prominent Christians, or on ground given by wealthy families, not themselves Christians, to their dependents, the work of burial would probably be undertaken by the Christian members of these households. Then, as the number of Christians increased, and the presence of tombs of martyrs rendered certain cemeteries popular, the task of burial became entrusted to professionals, to the *fossores* (*fossarii*) or diggers.

2

The work of these *fossores* extended from the preparation of surface graves, a subject on which all too little is known, to the excavation and even decoration of catacombs. An important stage in the organization of Christian cemeteries in Rome was reached when the Church itself took over the charge of a

2 A *fossor* (digger) from the cemetery of Callistus

cemetery, early in the third century. At that time Zephyrinus, Bishop of Rome, placed Callistus, later to be his successor, in charge 'of the cemetery', which is presumably that of San Callisto on the Via Appia Antica. About this time the Church of Rome was rent with controversies about discipline and doctrine between Callistus and Hippolytus, a Roman presbyter. In the latter's *Apostolic Tradition,* in which Hippolytus believed that he was setting out rules for Church government handed down from the Apostles, he states, 'no exorbitant charge shall be made for burial in the cemetery, for it belongs to all the poor, only the fee of the grave diggers and the cost of the tile [for closing the grave] shall be asked. The wages of the caretakers shall be paid by the bishop, lest any who go to that place be burdened.' It has been suggested that Hippolytus is having a hit at Callistus for his management of 'the cemetery'. However this may be, the passage shows that by *c.* 210–15 the Church was exercising supervision over the burial of all its members.

The numbers of workers involved in the construction and maintenance of cemeteries must have become very large. At Cirta, the capital of Numidia, in AD 303, when the local authorities were enforcing a recently issued edict of persecution, there were present at their interview with the clergy six *fossores* whose individual names are given, 'and the rest of them', whose names are not given.

But, before we consider the work of the *fossores*, the question may well be asked why the Christians went to the enormous toil of digging underground cemeteries. The Jews, at Rome for example, did the same thing, but their catacombs are not anterior in date to the Christian ones. However, the digging of catacombs by Christians is not a universal phenomenon, as in many places, including Rome, Christian cemeteries are found above ground. This was both a far easier method of burial, and the only possible one where the terrain was an obstacle to tunnelling. It was about the year AD 150 that a beginning was made in the long series of Christian catacombs, and the development of these was to continue for several hundred years. The idea of an underground tomb chamber (*hypogaeum*) was common in antiquity, and such chambers, dating from prehistoric times onwards, are particularly frequent in Sicily and Malta (pp. 138, 148, below). A development of sepulchral passages is infrequent. The nearest approach to it is a pagan burial place at Anzio, dating from the fourth and third centuries BC, and in North Africa there is at Sousse (Hadrumetum) a pagan catacomb called the catacomb of Agrippa, which was in use from about AD 230 to the beginning of the fourth century, and instances of burial passages may be found at the tomb of the Scipios, or at those of the Statilii and others at Rome.

The Christians started from the rock-cut sepulchre, closed with a stone, in which the body of Jesus was laid, and the earliest Christian underground tombs were probably no more than tomb chambers, such as were sometimes constructed by individual families even when catacombs existed.

The tombs of Christians, and in particular the tombs of martyrs, became centres of Christian resort. 'There [i.e. at the tomb of Polycarp] the Lord will permit us, as shall be possible to us, to assemble ourselves together in joy and gladness, and to celebrate the birthday of his martyrdom, alike in memory of them that have fought before, and for the training and preparation of those that are to fight hereafter.' So wrote the Church at Smyrna. The earliest reference to a Eucharist at a tomb is in the apocryphal Acts of John (*c.* 150), and, in the middle of the third century, we find Cyprian writing to his Church, 'We always as you remember offer sacrifice for them, as often as we celebrate the anniversary days of the martyrs by an annual commemoration.' Such reunions must have been virtually impossible as the numbers of Christians increased, and moreover, it became the desire of many to be buried in proximity to martyrs' tombs. Hence cemeteries were constructed, and the terrain round Rome and other places lent itself to the construction of these under the earth. In the persecution under Valerian (256–9) Christians were forbidden to visit cemeteries (*areae*). That was an official prohibition, but long before this, Christian cemeteries in North Africa were liable to be attacked and plundered by mobs, as Tertullian informs us. Valerian's prohibition was obviously directed against a practice common among Christians.

Burial within the walls of Rome was forbidden by law. By walls one means, for practical purposes, the Aurelian walls built about AD 270, which encompassed a far wider area than that enclosed by the Servian walls, reputed to go back to the distant period of the kings. Hence there are burial places, even Christian ones, inside the Aurelian circuit. But long before these walls were built the wealthier citizens had lined the roads leading from the city with their family tombs. The satirist Juvenal, writing in the early years of the second century AD, stated that the subject of his satire would be the dead, 'whose ashes the Flaminian and Latin ways conceal'. The most notable example of such tombs are those still standing for miles along the Via Appia Antica.

In the vicinity of Rome there are vast areas of the rock called *tufa*. There are three varieties of this, 'lithoidal' tufa used in building, non-cohesive tufa (*pozzolana*) from which, mixed with lime, the Romans made mortar, and a third variety, semi-cohesive, that in texture lies between the other two. The demand for *pozzolana* was great and quarries were dug from which it was extracted. These were called *arenaria*, a name that included not merely quarries, but passages of irregular shape and size. Such passages might form the nucleus of a catacomb constructed in the areas of semi-cohesive tufa, but *arenaria* are easily

3 *Pamphilus*. A passage with *loculi* intact. Parallel passages end abruptly, as here, showing that the limits of the property had been reached. Several *loculi* have been inserted across the end of the passage. They are now inaccessible, and indicate that the floor had been lowered to make room for more burials

distinguished from the latter, in which the passages would be far more carefully and regularly dug, on some sort of plan. Sometimes catacombs were constructed in the wrong kind of rock, e.g. the catacomb of Pontian at Rome, where the rock is sandstone, and strata of differing colours can clearly be seen at certain points, or in that of Valentinus where the rock is lithoidal tufa. But in other areas hard rock predominates, as in Sicily and Malta, and did not seriously inhibit the diggers. The influx of water, and the flooding caused by this was also a problem, which can again be best seen in the catacomb of Pontian where a pool of water may have become an underground baptistery in the fifth or sixth century. Pagans frequently made tombs in *arenaria* and occasionally a pagan tomb or tombs form the nucleus of, or are in close contiguity to a Christian cemetery. This contiguity may be explained in several ways; tombs may have been abandoned allowing the ground to fall into the possession of Christians, or families, originally pagan, may have become Christian. But whatever the reasons, pagan, Jewish and Christian tombs may occur almost side by side, and may indicate that in differing places and circumstances relations were not so bad as literary sources suggest: it is probable, for example, that pagan and Christian families shared the notable catacomb discovered in 1956 near the Via Latina (pp. 82, 124–8, below).

Cemeteries both above ground and underground were limited by the rights of property. Traces of such a limiting factor may be seen, for instance, in the catacomb of Pamphilus at Rome, where numerous passages end abruptly, and there clearly was no intention of carrying them farther, graves being even placed across the passages at their termination. But it is obvious from the extent of the cemeteries at Rome, Naples, Syracuse and Malta that Christians owned a large amount of property in the vicinity of cities, and that by the year 300 their numbers must have included numerous wealthy people.

4   The initial stage in the construction of a catacomb was to dig a tunnel into a hillside, perhaps from an abandoned quarry for *pozzolana*, or to make a stairway downward from the surface to the required depth. From such a beginning the making of the catacomb progressed, presumably according to some sort of plan, though we cannot always trace this. Passages were dug, generally at right angles to the original one, and these might lead into others parallel to the first passage. But deviations were sometimes necessary, as for instance where the diggers met with tufa of the wrong sort. Then construction continued downward

to a second, third, fourth and even fifth level, though sometimes this process was reversed, and a higher level was superposed on a lower one. From time to time light wells (*lucernaria* or *luminaria*) were dug which served both to let light into the catacomb, and to facilitate the removal to the surface of excavated material. These were furnished with footholds to enable a person to climb up or down, and in later times, even to this day, were the recipients of débris thrown from above. Contiguous catacombs might, in course of time become linked to each other, but on some occasions they were carefully left separate. A good example of the 'linking' process is to be found in the catacomb of Priscilla at Rome where several separate burial areas existed about the end of the second century, one connected with an *arenarium*, and another with the region of the *Cappella Greca* (p. 154, below). The *Cappella* was originally a separate tomb, and different regions had their own staircases for access. The *Cappella Greca* belonged to a rich family, but the tombs of the *region* of the *arenarium* are those of a Christian community. Thus by the end of the third century, the Christians owned a large property almost at the gates of Rome. That those buried in different areas belonged to different social classes is shown by the tomb of the Acilii, added to this complex sometime later. New entrances were also made particularly in order to render the tombs of martyrs more easy of access. The passages in the catacombs are normally about 7–10

4 Malta. Entrance to the catacomb at Tad-deyr (Rabat). The process of tunnelling into a hillside is well illustrated here. A church was built at the entrance, but this has long since disappeared

7

5 (*opposite*) *Domitilla*. A staircase linking upper and lower levels. *Loculi* were cut into the sides of the staircase to utilize all available space

6 *Praetextatus*. A light well, richly decorated. Note the *putti* harvesting olives

7 *Priscilla*. The *Cappella Greca*, so called from two Greek inscriptions found in it (see Ill. 129). In the apse may be seen the subject of Ill. 70. Note the stucco decoration to left, and the stone bench on which participants in a feast of remembrance would sit

feet high, and about 3–4 feet wide. But sometimes, to ease the task of extension, the floor of a passage would be lowered, and thus some passages are over 20 feet high; similarly much wider passages are also found, for example in the Jewish catacomb of the Vigna Randanini at Rome and in the catacombs at Naples and at Syracuse.

Next we must consider the actual graves, and the Latin vocabulary attached to them. The simplest type is a hollow dug into the wall (of a passage) in which the body, wrapped in linen, was laid lengthwise, parallel to the passage; the opening was then sealed with tiles, stones or marble which were sometimes re-used, being originally from pagan tombs, and placed back to front when put to Christian use. Such graves are called *loculi*. Sometimes they were made large enough to contain two, three or even more bodies, and occasionally there are grave pits, perhaps silent witnesses to a plague, to hold a number of bodies (*polyandri*). *Loculi* for two bodies sometimes bear two strokes on the cement outside to indicate the fact. In antiquity the mortality of infants and children was tragically high, and we can see this from the number of little *loculi*, often placed together near the corners of passages. Some graves bear brief inscriptions, or have recognition signs, such as a coin or coins sunk in the cement surrounding the covering, or a child's toy. In the passages numerous oil lamps were cemented in, and also vases for perfume. There are few passages where the graves have not been opened in the search for relics and valuable objects: a notable example of an untouched passage is to be found in the catacomb of Commodilla, and there are others in the catacombs of Pamphilus and Novatian.

But besides the simple *loculi* there are numerous *cubicula*, or tomb chambers in which a whole family could find its resting place over a considerable period. These correspond to the family tombs erected along the roads near Rome. The *cubicula* are variously shaped, but in general are rectangular, and about 100 to 150 square feet in area. Burials took place in the walls and sometimes in the floor. Graves made in the floors of *cubicula*, or of passages, are called *formae*. Occasionally room was made for more burials, as in passages, by raising the ceiling or lowering the floor. In the *cubicula* frequently, and less often in the passages, more elaborate tombs are found called *arcosolia*, as in Illustration 8. The shape of these enabled graves to be placed in the curved wall under the arch, or on or under the shelf (*mensa*) below it. Also used were stone coffins (*solia*) which could be placed on the

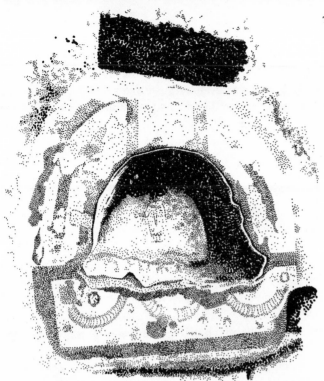

8 An *arcosolium* at Syracuse, decorated with painted patterns: a *loculus* above

shelf under the arch; occasionally existing paintings were ruined by the insertion of a new *loculus*. It is in the *cubicula* and the *arcosolia* that the bulk of the catacomb paintings are to be found. Some *cubicula* had engaged pillars at their entrance or within them, some had a triangular gable and some were closed with doors.

There are few rooms of any size dating from the centuries of persecution in the catacombs. As examples of larger rooms one may cite the Crypt of the Popes in the catacomb of St Callistus at Rome, in which third-century bishops of Rome were buried, the *basilichetta*, about 20 metres long, in the catacomb of St Hippolytus, the large circular crypts in the catacomb of San Giovanni at Syracuse, extensive areas in San Gennaro at Naples, and perhaps a room or open space in St Paul's catacomb in Malta. But at Rome there is no room in which the early Christians could *habitually* have worshipped, in the centuries of persecution, though it is equally clear that in certain localities gatherings to commemorate the dead, whether martyrs or relatives, took place. An interesting example of this is found in the inscription of Aelia Secundula, who died in North Africa in AD 299; this records that her children set up a *mensa* or table at her tomb, where a meal took place, at which her relatives recounted her praises.

19

Some tombs in surface cemeteries were covered by a roof supported by pillars, in other words by a *baldacchino* (*tegurium* or *ciborium*), and this form was transferred to underground tombs. Actually only one example has been found at Rome, in the catacomb of Peter and Marcellinus, but this type of tomb is found frequently in Malta and also at Acrae and other sites in Sicily (See Chapter 8).

In every catacomb the marks made by the picks of the *fossores* can be clearly seen. These may serve as a reminder of the enormous amount of work involved in the construction of catacombs. Owing to the confined space it would be impossible for more than one or two persons to work together at a time.

We know what *fossores* looked like from the pictures of them still extant in various catacombs. They wear a short tunic and carry a pick and a lamp, and even a basket or bag for excavated material. The lamp is furnished with a chain, to which there may be attached a spike which could be driven into the wall, so as to leave the *fossor* with both hands free.

The organization of the *fossores* must have been one of considerable complexity, but it is likely that they became individually attached to the staff of a particular cemetery. Inscriptions found at Sant' Agnese point to a whole family of *fossores* there. We have already seen that they formed a numerous group at Cirta in AD 303. They appear there, along with the clergy, in a context that has nothing to do with cemeteries, and the problem arises whether they were regarded as clergy or not. In the Theodosian Code, in two edicts of AD 360 and 357, we find them mentioned, not as *fossores* (Latin) but as *kopiatae* (Greek), i.e. toilers. 'Clerics and those persons whom recent usage has begun to call gravediggers' are exempted from public duties in the first of these edicts; in the second, assimilated to the clergy, they are exempted from a certain tax. By AD 400 'they protect themselves by the title of clergy' and in that year we have exemption from military service refused to those who 'protecting themselves by the title of clerics are occupied in the gloomy obsequies for the dead', i.e. certain shirkers were insinuating themselves into an exempt class. Finally, in AD 447 we find the emperor Valentinian III imposing severe penalties on clergy who plunder tombs, and that systematically (!); while even bishops are not exempt from this charge, these plunderers may well in general be *fossores*, whose opportunities for such conduct, if they were disposed toward it, must have been extensive. To give one instance: with the passage of time and the extinction of

2

families, passages and *cubicula* became abandoned and derelict. Into such was piled rubbish excavated from other parts of the catacomb, to save the arduous task of taking it to the surface, and temptation to rob may have been too great. Abandoned *loculi* might also be emptied and re-sold.

When one of the *fossores* at Cirta was asked his profession he replied, *artifex*, craftsman. This may introduce us to a wider aspect of the *fossor*'s task, which would include the carving of inscriptions, and the decoration, particularly of *cubicula* and *arcosolia*, with paintings. Differences in style of lettering have been noted in different cemeteries, and inscriptions of uncertain provenance have been identified by their style. The same sort of criterion can be applied to paintings, where the colour schemes in one cemetery differ notably from those in another. But no pictures have yet been found of workmen or craftsmen at work other than the *fossores*. Nor is there any reference to a catacomb painter in any extant literary source (but cf. p. 22, below). The funerary inscription of a painter has been found in the Jewish catacomb near the Via Appia Antica (Vigna Randanini); this catacomb does not lack painted decoration, but whether *this* painter took part in it is quite unknown to us.

Other references in inscriptions to the profession of painter indicate, from the names of the persons concerned, that they were freedman or slaves. Three Christians from the fourth century have been found among them:

(1) AURELIUS FELIX PICT (OR)
    CL ANTONIO ET (SYAGRIO CONSS.) [i.e. AD 382]
This probably closed a *loculus*.

(2) LOCUS PRISCI PICTORIS, 'the burial place of the painter Priscus'. This came from the catacomb of Cyriaca, and was re-used in the building of the basilica of St Laurence. The stone had been twice used already, the inscription on its other side being LOCUS IUS(TINI).

(3) An inscription, seen complete by Marangoni in the eighteenth century from St Callistus, half of which has perished.
    FELICI FILIO BENEMERENTI QUI VIXIT ANNOS
    XXIII DIES X QUI EXIVIT VIRGO DE SAECULO ET
    NEOFITUS IN PACE
    PARENTES FECERUNT
    DEP III NON AUG

As can be seen on the extant portion, there are depicted a painter's tools, compasses, stylus and two brushes. But whether these were ever used on a catacomb wall we cannot now know. Jerome, in praising the virtues of the presbyter Nepotian,[2] relates that he decorated the basilicas of the Church and the chapels of the martyrs with different flowers, leaves and bunches of grapes. This brings him near to catacomb painting, but Nepotian cannot be regarded as more than a dilettante.

The *fossores* may also have acted as keepers of the cemeteries. One inscription identifies the work of a *topophylax* (guardian of a place) with that of a *fossor*. At their head must have been a *mensor* to co-ordinate the work of digging, and to plan future operations. Such a one may have been Diogenes, whose portrait – the principal decoration of a *cubiculum* – was seen and copied by Boldetti (1663–1749); it is now irretrievably damaged. The word *fossor* (*fosrus*) appears also in inscriptions TROFIMUS FOSRO, IUNIUS FOSSOR AVENTINUS. Diehl gives nine examples of funeral inscriptions of *fossores*.

In AD 366 the *fossores* took part with gladiators and charioteers in the bloody disturbances that attended the election of Damasus as Bishop of Rome. A body of hardy workmen, they must have been valuable as rioters. While their activity throws a distasteful light on a degenerating spirit among Christians, it is interesting to note that at Alexandria, towards the beginning of the fifth century, a similar well defined group, the *parabolani* or attendants of the sick, played a turbulent role and had to be restrained.

In the pontificate of Julius I (337–52) a change in the status of *fossores* begins to be apparent. Two inscriptions of that period refer to a *fossor* Alexander, from whom individuals bought graves in the cemetery of Marcus and Marcellianus. The same circumstance concerns the purchase of a place in the cemetery of Commodilla (A LA)UR FOSSOREM, or in the cemetery of St Cyriaca where in AD 405 a certain Eurialus placed his tomb AD MENSAM MARTYRIS LAURENTII DESCENDENTIBUS IN CRYPTA PARTE DEXTRA DE FOSSORE . . . (L) OCI IPSIUS.

There was a certain competition for good places, near martyrs, and a mutilated inscription refers to a *fossor* digging a grave for himself near such a favoured spot. In the catacomb of St Callistus we find that Serpentius bought a grave from the *fossor* Quintus near St Cornelius, SERPENTIUS EMIT LOCUM A QUINTO FOSSORE AD SANTUM CORNELIUM. From

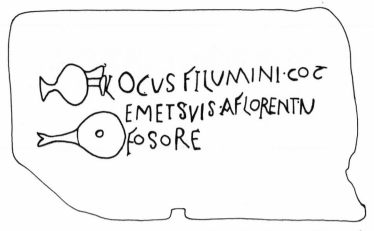

9 Inscription showing the purchase of a tomb from a *fossor*: it reads (in illiterate Latin): 'the place of Filumenus, which he bought for his family from the *fossor* Florentius'

AD 391 to *c.* 440 there is a series of inscriptions recording such sales by *fossores* of places in or near catacombs, and the right to sell places prepared by a *fossor* passed to his heirs. Nor were the sales haphazard. Even the price is occasionally mentioned on the inscriptions. The documents were preserved in an office (?*statio*), and could be inspected there: the inscriptions would be but a summary of the documents, of which, written on waxed tablets or papyrus, it is unlikely that any example will turn up. The sale was witnessed: 'in the presence of all the *fossores*', 'in the presence of Severus and Laurentius, *fossores*', as two inscriptions record. Diehl gives 19 examples of such purchases from *fossores*.

An interesting example of funerary arrangements is found in the cemetery of Commodilla from the end of the fourth century. The *fossor* Projecticius is mentioned on two inscriptions as selling places. One of these, the *locus* of Zosimus and Concordia was bought in 398, probably at the death of Concordia, and an inscribed stone inserted. Zosimus, now aged about 70, died in 402(?) and a new stone was inserted to record this. As the available space was not big enough, the earlier stone was split in two in order to make room, and the unwanted portion used to close a *loculus* in another gallery, where it was found.

But this period of control by the *fossores* did not last for long. The last mention of a *fossor* is about the year 430. After that date the tombs, more and more placed within churches or in surface cemeteries, became assigned by *prepositi* or *mansionarii*, and the ancient *fossores* disappear from history; the modern *fossores* are the corps of workmen who are now engaged on works of conservation and restoration, and who can guide the visitor in long walks through the ancient passages.

2
The History of the Catacombs in Antiquity

When I was a boy at Rome, and was being educated in liberal studies, I was accustomed, with others of like age and mind, to visit on Sundays the sepulchres of the apostles and martyrs. And often did I enter the crypts, deep dug in the earth, with their walls on either side lined with the bodies of the dead, where everything is so dark that it almost seems as if the psalmist's words were fulfilled: *Let them go down alive into hell* (*Ps.* 55.15). Here and there the light, not entering through windows, but filtering down from above through shafts, relieves the horror of the darkness. But again, as one cautiously moves forward, the black night closes round, and there comes to the mind the line of Vergil:

> Surrounding horrors all my soul affright
> And more, the dreadful silence of the night.[3]

> Jerome.

There was once a wide-spread idea that the early Christians habitually worshipped in the catacombs, and also hid there in time of danger. This idea is, however, generally speaking, erroneous. As has been already mentioned, there are no large rooms in the catacombs built in the centuries of persecution that are capable of holding many worshippers, and in any case, the distance of the burial places from the city would make the walk into the country and back, perhaps in the early morning, a time-consuming and exhausting process. Christians may have hid in the catacombs, but there is nothing to prove it. Moreover, it can now be shown that in the third century (whatever may have been the case in the time of Justin Martyr, in the middle of the second century) the Christians possessed places of worship in central Rome more practical for meeting than the damp and narrow galleries of the suburban cemeteries.[4]

But as the passage from Jerome cited at the head of this chapter shows, Christians did frequent catacombs, particularly to visit the tombs of martyrs, and of their own families. Several rooms, such as the *Cappella Greca* in St Priscilla, the cult centre at St Sebastian, the crypts of the popes and of St Cecilia at St Callistus, and the *basilichetta* in the *Coemeterium Maius* (not to

10,11

mention areas in the catacombs of Naples, Malta and Syracuse) are unmistakably centres for the reunion of Christians.

As mentioned in the previous chapter, burials in catacombs began towards the middle of the second century. In themselves the catacombs have little literary history, and hardly any important events about them are recorded in our extant literary sources. The names of some catacombs or of areas in catacombs probably are derived from a member of the family that owned the ground, e.g. Priscilla or Domitilla, or Praetextatus or Lucina; others are named from martyrs buried there, e.g. Agnes, Pancratius, Peter (not the Apostle) and Marcellinus, or Lucia at Syracuse: other names arose from topographical indications, such as the expression *ad catacumbas* itself, *ad clivum cucumeris* (cucumber hill), *ad septem palumbas* (seven pigeons), or *ad duas lauros* (at the two laurel trees), as the cemetery of Peter and Marcellinus was also called.

Two notable exceptions to these forms of names are the *Coemeterium Maius*, so called perhaps to distinguish it from a neighbouring cemetery which may be Sant' Agnese, but is more likely to be some other, now unidentified, and St Callistus named after the person 'put in charge of the cemetery' by Zephyrinus, Bishop of Rome *c.* AD 210. The cemetery was obviously already in existence, but whether it had a name we do not know. The fact that it is called 'the cemetery', without any other designation,

10 *Callistus*. Crypt of the Popes, in which third-century bishops of Rome were buried (cf. also Ill. 11). In centre, the inscription of Damasus, *c.* 380

11 *Callistus*. Crypt of the
Popes. Inscription in
Greek lettering for
Pontian, bishop from 230
to 235. The letters MP
(martyr) were added by a
later hand

12 Circular crypt in San
Giovanni at Syracuse.
The sarcophagus of
Adelfia (see Ill. 35) was
found in one of these
crypts

13 Catacomb of San
Gennaro at Naples. Crypt
of the Bishops

may indicate that this was, when Hippolytus wrote (*c.* 225), the cemetery which was the particular care and property of the Roman Church. We may note in passing, that Zephyrinus himself was not buried there. According to the *Liber Pontificalis* he was buried 'in his own cemetery, adjoining the cemetery of Callistus, on the Via Appia'; according to the *Notitia Ecclesiarum* (see p. 46, below), he was buried in a surface cemetery, and not underground. According to the *De Locis sanctis martyrum* (p. 46, below), the martyr Tarcisius was buried in the same tomb. Where the ground was originally owned by an individual or a family, there would be a tendency for such cemeteries to pass over to the control of the Church, and attachments were made from the late third or early fourth centuries onwards between cemeteries and the *tituli* or parishes of Rome. In the previous chapter we have seen how for a period in the late fourth and early fifth centuries, the *fossores* had temporarily considerable power in the cemeteries. But two inscriptions, from the catacomb of Domitilla and Callistus respectively, show clergy with authority, and one of these inscriptions can be dated to *c.* 296–304. 'Alexius and Capriola made [this tomb] in their own lifetime, by permission (*iussu*) of the presbyters Archelaus and Dulcitius'; 'The deacon Severus made a double *cubiculum* with *arcosolia* and a light well as a quiet resting place in peace for himself and his family by permission (*iussu*) of his pope Marcellinus.' In official language of the third and fourth centuries *iussu* indicates the permission of a superior authority, even of the emperor himself, and it is clear from this case that the highest authority in the Church could intervene in a matter pertaining to one individual and his family.

Of the names of catacombs mentioned in the preceding paragraphs, the only one that need detain us at the moment is that of (Flavia) Domitilla, niece of the emperor Domitian (AD 81–96), and wife of her cousin Flavius Clemens, consul in 95. Their two children were destined for succession to the Empire, but in this same year (95) Clemens and other prominent Romans were victims of the 'reign of terror' that marked the closing period of Domitian's rule. The reasons for their fall, according to the late epitome of the history of Cassius Dio, were 'atheism and Jewish customs', an expression which may lead us to suppose that they were Christians. Clemens was executed, Domitilla banished. She is regarded as a Christian by, amongst others, Eusebius, the earliest Church historian, and by Christian tradition generally. However, the question of the religion of these noble Romans does not really concern us here. The naming of a catacomb after Domitilla proves nothing more than that the Christians about AD 150 had begun to construct this vast catacomb under land that had at one time belonged to Domitilla, as surface inscriptions show, and which was already by that date the site of an extensive surface cemetery. The nomenclature, 'Crypt of the Flavians', applied to a portion of the catacomb, is purely hypothetical, as the surviving inscription of a certain Flavius Sabinus and his sister Titiana may have been thrown into the crypt from the débris of the surface cemetery. The Crypt of the Flavians may be of second-century date, but whether it was, from its inception, a Christian burial place, is not absolutely certain. We need not delay over the tantalizing fragmentary inscription – RUM-IORUM in which the words *sepulcrum Flaviorum* have hopefully been seen. Anyhow by the fourth century other saints and martyrs took their place alongside, or superseded, Domitilla. These martyrs are Petronella, a legendary daughter of St Peter, and Nereus and Achilleus, who were honoured in a semi-subterranean basilica built in the fourth century.

14 The 'tantalizing inscription' from the Crypt of the Flavians

The catacomb of Priscilla, on the other side of the city on the Via Salaria Nuova, contains the crypt of the Acilii Glabriones. This calls to mind another of Domitian's victims, Acilius Glabrio, consul in AD 91. The inscriptions that identify this crypt are however much later than the reign of Domitian, and are, religiously speaking, neutral, apart from one Christian inscription of the third century. It appears too, that this crypt may also have served as a water reservoir and that the inscriptions may have come from elsewhere in this complex of surface and subterranean tombs.

In the early third century the 'Crypt of the Popes' was developed in the cemetery of St Callistus, which was the burial place of bishops of Rome from Pontian (d. 235) to Miltiades (d. 314), with the exception of Marcellinus (d. 304) and Marcellus (d. 309). Other bishops of Rome, not buried in the crypt, but elsewhere in St Callistus, were Cornelius (d. 253), Gaius (d. 296) and Eusebius (d. 310). It would be hazardous to suggest under whom the building of the crypt began, but its original date must surely fall between the appointment of Callistus to superintend 'the cemetery', and the first burial therein. Now, Pontian died in exile in Sardinia, whither he had been sent along with his schismatic rival Hippolytus. The relics of both were brought back to Rome, but those of Hippolytus were taken, we may

10

presume, to the cemetery near the Via Tiburtina which bears his name, and in which his statue – now standing in the entrance to the Vatican library – was found in the sixteenth century.

But it can be assumed that the burial of Anteros, bishop for a brief space in 236, was the earliest in the crypt. He can hardly, however, have instituted it, and its preparation to receive the bodies of the Roman bishops probably took place in the period of peace marked by the reign of Alexander Severus (222–35). But the area known as the Crypt of Lucina, now joined to, but originally separate from the catacomb of Callistus, is earlier than the latter, and represents a development of Christian cemeteries in the later second century. It is in this crypt that Cornelius was buried, probably about 258. 15

The years c. 200 to c. 260 would seem to mark a crucial period in the development not only of the catacombs but of the organization of the Church at Rome. In the *Liber Pontificalis*, which contains biographies of the popes, and of which the earlier part is of the sixth century, it is stated of Fabian, bishop from 236 to 250, that 'he divided the regions of the city among the deacons . . . and ordered many buildings (*fabricae*) to be made throughout the cemeteries'. Whether these cemeteries were on the surface or underground is not indicated, but the same word (*fabricae*) is used in the Filocalian Calendar of 354 for the churches built by Julius I (337–52). We learn also that Fabian took great care to arrange to collect the acts of martyrs, and perhaps their relics also, as those of Pontian and Hippolytus were 16 probably brought back from Sardinia about this time. All this points to a growing interest in martyrs and their anniversaries, and consequently in their tombs. It is also clear that by c. 300 the Christians had begun to erect commemorative buildings in the surface cemeteries, as is evidenced by the surviving remains 17 above the catacomb of St Callistus of a *cella trichorus*, 'which had semi-circular niches each surrounded by a half-dome'.[5] In such a building Zephyrinus may have been buried about 217.

After the persecution under Decius, in which Fabian perished, a determined attack on the Church took place under the emperor Valerian in 257–8. He did not persecute indiscriminately, but attacked important and wealthy Christians, both clergy and laity, and also imperial officials and servants. As we know both from Egypt and North Africa, Christians were forbidden to visit the cemeteries, and it is clear from the edict of restitution issued by Gallienus when he called off the persecution (261), that cemeteries had been seized.

About the time of the persecution under Valerian, however, two significant events occurred. In the first place the martyrdom of Sixtus II of Rome took place *in cimiterio*, where he was arrested with various members of his clergy including Laurence, his chief deacon, on 6 August 258. Four of his seven deacons were executed with Sixtus, and Laurence shortly afterwards, perhaps reserved for more searching preliminaries because of his knowledge of the Church's finances. Why Sixtus went to the cemetery is not known. He may have gone with his clergy to hide, he may have gone to preside at some commemoration. Nor do we know whether the Latin expression means 'in a cemetery', or 'in the cemetery': in the latter case it could refer most appropriately to St Callistus. In any case, as Sixtus was found *in cimiterio*, whither Christians had been prohibited from going, he was putting himself in danger of arrest. Another of his deacons was named Januarius and in 1904 there was found near the crypt of St Cecilia a fragmentary inscription IANOY(APIUS). But whether this marked the tomb of the martyred deacon we cannot now tell.

The other event presents us with a puzzle which there is absolutely no means, on our present evidence, of solving. As was mentioned in the previous chapter, there grew up, from the second half of the third century, at the site where the basilica of St Sebastian now stands on the Via Appia Antica, a centre of veneration of the Apostles Peter and Paul. Now the bodies of the two Apostles had long been in their tombs, the one on the Vatican Hill, the other on the road to Ostia. The existence of this cult centre on the Via Appia, to which numerous (640 in all) *graffiti* at the site testify, is most perplexing. The *graffiti* also, if

Opposite

15 (*left*) *Callistus*. The tomb of Cornelius, Bishop of Rome (d. in exile in 253). Above are fragments of the commemorative verses by Damasus

16 (*right*) *Hippolytus*. Entrance to the basilica: this is not the original entrance, but belongs to a restoration of the sixth century in the time of Pope Vigilius (537–55)

17 (*below*) One of the *cellae trichori* near the catacomb of Callistus (after restoration of the upper portion). A *cella trichorus* was a building with three apses. These buildings were used for funerary purposes, and were, at the period of the excavations in the nineteenth century, surrounded by surface graves

18 *St Sebastian. Graffiti* invoking the Apostles Peter and Paul. The principal one shown here reads PAUL ED(T) PETRE PETITE PRO VICTORE ('Paul and Peter pray for Victor')

we may judge from the names of those who wrote them and the expressions that they used, are the scratchings of visitors, not of Romans. 'These *graffiti* constitute one of the best documents to demonstrate how much the devotion towards the founders of the Roman Church had penetrated even to the humblest social classes of the Christian world in the second half of the third century.'[6] This site too must be the one to which Jerome refers, as it is the only one where 'sepulchres of the apostles' would be associated with a catacomb. This is probably also the *martyrium* of the Apostles visited by Ammonius, a monk who accompanied Athanasius *c.* 340, when the latter was in exile in the West.

Some think that, in 258, in the persecution under Valerian, the bodies of the Apostles were moved, for reasons of safety, from the pagan cemeteries of the Vatican and the Via Ostiensis, and that they were taken back to their original tombs when permanent peace came in the early fourth century. That a festival of the Apostles began *ad catacumbas* in that year is a possible deduction from the above-mentioned Filocalian Calendar, where we find the date of AD 258 associated with such a celebration. The numerous *graffiti* invoking the two Apostles attest the festival's existence, though the date of these *graffiti* may be later. But in any case, when the *Basilica Apostolorum* was built in the fourth century, the floor of the basilica covered the site, and the manner of the festival must have been altered.

By the sixth century one account of the institution of the celebration was that disciples from the East, whence the Apostles had originally come, stole their bodies after execution, but were able to carry them only as far as the site *ad catacumbas*, where a violent thunderstorm so discomfited the thieves that they left their booty. Another account puts things the other way round and makes the translation of their bodies from the site to their present tombs in the time of Cornelius of Rome (251–3)! When Damasus wrote verses for the site, as for many others connected with martyrs, the sense of them is: 'Whoever you are who seeks the names of Peter and Paul, you ought to know that here formerly the saints [i.e. Peter and Paul] dwelt (*Hic habitasse* (v.l. *habitare*) *prius*). The East sent the disciples – that we willingly admit – and by the shedding of their blood they followed Christ through the stars and have sought their home on high. Rome rather [i.e. than any other city] deserved to claim them as her citizens. May Damasus declare these words to praise you that now are stars!'[7] We do not know where this inscription was placed at the site.

'Here formerly the saints dwelt' – in life or in death? It is more likely to be the latter, as the whole circumstances of the veneration point to a remembrance of the dead in an area which already had many pagan tombs. But if we accept the past sense of *habitasse*, it looks as though this cult was on its way out when Damasus wrote. It is interesting to note that the hymn *Apostolorum Passio*, ascribed to Ambrose, mentions the three sites where the Apostles were venerated, but the hymn of Prudentius (AD 403) on the same subject has no mention of the festival at St Sebastian.

It is possible that around the middle of the third century veneration of the Apostles, owing to the growing number of Christians, had become impossible in the crowded areas of their original tombs: the excavations under St Peter's amply reveal the congested surroundings of the apostolic *aedicula* in the Vatican cemetery. The newly constituted shrine *ad Catacumbas* may have possessed relics attributed to the Apostles, just as happened at Milan in the time of Ambrose (bishop in AD 374–97), where in the Basilica of the Apostles at Milan, according to Ambrose's biographer Paulinus, 'relics of St Peter and St Paul had recently been deposited with great and universal devotion'.[8]

The church built at the site in the fourth century was called *Basilica Apostolorum*. But the relics of Sebastian, a martyr in the time of Diocletian were transferred there in that very century, and so the site got its permanent name. This shows that the celebration in honour of the Apostles was rapidly being forgotten, and so it remained until the archaeological discoveries of the last century. The shrine of the Apostles was independent of the catacomb that developed at the site. What role was played in all this by the villas that are contiguous must continue to intrigue (and mystify) visitors and investigators, but the exploration of the catacomb of San Gennaro at Naples shows the abodes of living and dead in close contiguity.

During the second half of the third century there must have been a vast development of catacombs. For instance in the catacomb of Novatian, in which the relics of the former schismatic (d. *c.* 258 in exile) were interred, we find inscriptions dated from 266 and 270, and we find that by the early years of the fourth century a now nameless catacomb at the Villa Doria Pamphili on the Via Aurelia Antica was reaching an advanced stage of construction. This is proved by a *graffito* mentioning the emperor Maxentius, which must be dated around AD 310, 19

19 Inscription from
catacomb at the Villa
Doria Pamphili, with
reference to Maxentius; at
bottom (M)AXI(MU)S
INCLUSUS EST III
IDUS OCT., and a
(damaged) Constantinian
monogram (with AO)

accompanying which is a Chi-rho monogram, before its use by Constantine.

It is hard to say what effect the Great Persecution that began in 303 had on the catacombs. A great deal of Christian property was confiscated as, once again, we learn from the edict of restitution – the so-called 'Edict of Milan' of 313 – but cemeteries are not on this occasion specifically mentioned. However unreliable details about the lives of the popes given in the *Liber Pontificalis* of the sixth century may be, it is not without interest that the cemeteries are mentioned several times with regard to the later third and early fourth centuries, and that in a way not inapposite to the period. Dionysius, bishop from 259 to 268, is stated to have made regulations for the cemeteries and episcopal sees under his jurisdiction: that would indicate reorganization after the persecution under Valerian. Felix I (270–5) is stated to have instituted celebrations of mass at the tombs of martyrs. We shall see that this custom was extensively practised in the late fourth century, but the reference to Felix is not explicit as to the extent of this practice at its first institution. If the statement about his successor Eutychian (275–83) – that he buried 342 martyrs – is true, it would indicate that multiplication of the number of martyrs had begun. But, as Duchesne remarked in editing the *Liber Pontificalis*, 'we do not possess all the stories that circulated at Rome, from the fourth to the seventh century, on the martyrs and their sanctuaries'.[9]

The notice about Caius (283–96), contains obvious error. It refers to him as living in catacombs (*cryptae*) in order to avoid the persecution under Diocletian. But this persecution did not begin till seven years after his death, and this attachment of Caius to a period of persecution is an example of a desire in the sixth century to bring bishops of Rome into such a connexion. His epitaph has been found, in fragments, in the catacomb of Callistus, but not in the Papal Crypt, and there has also been found an inscription in which is mentioned, if we may accept the reconstruction of De Rossi, the acquisition of an *arcosolium* near his tomb.

In 303 the storm of persecution broke, and the bishop of that time, Marcellinus (296–304) seems to have compromised himself by some real or apparent compliance with the demand that scriptures be surrendered, a lapse for which he atoned by subsequent repentance and martyrdom. He was buried in the cemetery of Priscilla on the Via Salaria by the good offices of a presbyter Marcellus and other clergy. His burial there may have been caused by a too inquisitive official surveillance of the cemetery of Callistus, particularly as his body and those of other martyrs had been forbidden burial by the authorities. One inscription from St Callistus has been mentioned above, in which Marcellinus had sponsored the making of a tomb with *arcosolia* and a light well by the deacon Severus, 'for himself and his family'.

After the death of Marcellinus the see remained vacant for several years, during which it is possible that the above-mentioned Marcellus acted as administrator till 308, when he became bishop. Systematic persecution was now ended under the rule of the usurper Maxentius, but the actions of Marcellus in reorganization, and disagreements within the Church over the treatment of lapsed Christians, led to his arrest and death from subsequent ill-treatment.

Things were similar under Eusebius, the next pope (308–9). He died in exile in Sicily, and was buried in the cemetery of Callistus, but not in the Papal Crypt, which seems to have gone out of use for good. A few fragments of the original inscription put up in his honour by Damasus have been found.

In the time of his successor Miltiades (311–14) the end of persecution was in sight, and confiscated property was being restored. Nearly one hundred years later this event was recalled in Augustine's controversy with the Donatist schismatics, who, in the war of documents that then ensued, referred to an account in which Miltiades was stated to have sent deacons with letters from the emperor (usurper) Maxentius and the Praetorian Prefect to the Prefect of the City, to recover confiscated property which Maxentius had ordered to be returned. This shows that, before his overthrow, Maxentius, who had already ceased to persecute, was also ingratiating himself with the Christians – perhaps even competing for their support – when the 'show-down' with Constantine took place. But events moved too fast, and Constantine's victory, followed by the 'Edict of Milan', put toleration on a permanent footing.

A great period of extension and development followed, both in the numbers of converts and in the extent and importance of Christian buildings. Miltiades was the last pope to be buried in

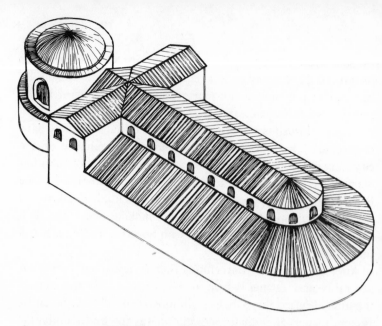

20 The cemetery church
at the catacomb of SS.
Peter and Marcellinus,
which was attached to the
circular tomb of Helena,
mother of Constantine

the cemetery of Callistus. Twenty years later his successor Silvester was buried in a basilica built at the cemetery of Priscilla. This event we can take as marking the beginning of the era of the building of churches in the cemeteries, in particular to 20 commemorate martyrs. These could be large edifices, such as the already mentioned *Basilica Apostolorum*, or that of Peter and Marcellinus adjoining the tomb of Helena, mother of Constantine, or that of Nereus and Achilleus at the cemetery of Domitilla. As examples of smaller cemetery churches containing the relics of martyrs one may cite those on the Via Ostiensis, at the cemeteries of Commodilla and Thecla. In the case of the latter it is possible that the little basilica in which a martyr was buried marks the commencement, and not the culmination of the catacomb. But in the case of Hippolytus we have the 16 underground basilica still surviving, with its quite imposing brick portal of the sixth century, in which are sockets that obviously held the hinges of the doors. The tomb was presumably in the apse, at the back of which, as well as in the side walls of the basilica, there are passages leading into the adjoining catacomb. Of greater significance than all these, however, were the churches built by Constantine not at catacombs, but at the tombs of the Apostles Peter and Paul. The cemetery churches became themselves called *coemeteria* because of the graves in, around or below them.

Meanwhile in the reorganization that took place, the individual cemeteries were bound more closely to the *tituli* (or parishes) of Rome; it may not be going too far to say that by 312 every *titulus* had its cemetery or portion of a cemetery. This process of organization may go back, in its initiation, to the time of Fabian, and must be connected with the rituals and gatherings in the cemeteries, under the control and presidency of the parochial clergy. Julius I (337–52) was a great builder of churches, three of which were connected with catacombs, i.e. at St Felix (*ad insalsatos* or *infulatos* – the meaning is uncertain), St Valentine on the Via Flaminia and Calepodius on the Via Aurelia Antica, where he himself was buried, but in a surface grave, not in the catacomb.

The transference of the relics of martyrs to fitting tombs had long been recognized, e.g. in the bringing back to Rome of those of Fabian and Hippolytus, who had died in Sardinia (above, p. 28) or of Cornelius who had died at Centumcellae (above, p. 29). The possible translation of the relics of St Peter and St Paul to the site *ad Catacumbas* is also a case in point. But in AD 386 we find an edict of Gratian, Valentinian II and Theodosius I forbidding the transference of buried bodies, and, in particular, forbidding interference with bodies of martyrs, but allowing the building of *martyria* at their tombs, i.e. of buildings in which they could be commemorated. This was an effort to stem what might have become an abuse, and, in fact, Roman custom long prohibited the removal of martyrs.

The festivals of the martyrs attracted throngs of visitors. The poet Prudentius, writing towards the year AD 400, has given an account of the multitudes who assembled, not from Rome only, but from various parts of Italy, at the tomb of the martyr Hippolytus, the memory of whose schism had completely faded, and whose death, by a curious twist of Christian imagination, had become assimilated to that of Hippolytus, son of Theseus, as narrated in, for example, the *Hippolytus* of Euripides. Prudentius saw, at Rome, 'innumerable tombs of martyrs'; he wrote poems on the passions of the Apostles Peter and Paul, and of the Roman martyrs Laurence, Hippolytus and Agnes. But of these poems the only one dealing with a catacomb is that on Hippolytus. He gives a good account of what it was (and is) to enter the many passages with their *lucernaria*: next to the martyr's tomb was an altar where mass was celebrated, such a one perhaps as can still be seen in the catacomb of Pamphilus. There was also a picture of the martyrdom, of which the poet gives a lurid description, in such detail that the representation may be considered to be in several scenes, as was commonly done in depicting, for example, the story of Jonah. The picture of

26

21 *Domitilla*. Decapitation of St Achilleus; a relief on a pillar preserved in the basilica of SS. Nereus and Achilleus. Between the figures of victim and executioner is a wreathed cross

Hippolytus had no historical value, save as an example of a poet's imagination working both on a painter's imagination, and, directly or indirectly, on a tragedian's. The scene is drawn ultimately from Euripides' *Hippolytus*.[10]

Representations of martyrdoms are not common in early Christian art. Notable examples are found at Rome in the relief representing the decapitation of Achilleus in the basilica of S. Nereus and Achilleus at the catacomb of Domitilla, and in a picture in the Roman house under the basilica of SS. John and Paul, of the decapitation of Crispin, Crispinian and Benedicta. These, however, do not compare with the horrid scenes described by Prudentius, for which one may find a fitting parallel in the far later pictures (sixteenth-seventeenth century) that 'decorate' San Stefano Rotondo. In Eastern Christianity we find St Basil the Great exhorting artists to represent the martyrdom of St Barlaam, and St Gregory of Nyssa describing the martyrdom of St Theodore, represented in a picture or pictures.

The fame of the martyrs grew as the threat of martyrdom receded. This happened not at Rome alone but also, for example, at Syracuse, where an inscription refers to the festival of 'My lady Lucia', a victim of the persecution under Diocletian, and now patron saint of the city. One effect of the devotion paid to martyrs was that new entrances were made to catacombs to provide better access to their tombs, as in the catacomb of Peter and Marcellinus, in which also the walls of passages adjoining their tomb were plastered.

More *lucernaria* were constructed, to afford an easier access. There was also great competition to be buried near martyrs. An inscription of the year 386 reads, 'He received a tomb near the threshold of the saints, a thing that many desire and few attain.' The desire to be buried close to a martyr was motivated by the idea that the martyr, who had attained the bliss of heaven, could help others to attain this bliss, the whole process being aided by the prayers of the living who assembled at these spots. These alterations led to the destruction of many other tombs.

We find that in the cemetery of Calepodius in Trastevere, a new staircase was constructed to afford easy access to the tomb of Callistus (d. *c.* 222) and this construction caused the filling of passages and the abandonment of part of that catacomb.

Similar alterations were carried out also at St Callistus, where numerous bodies were removed and buried in an ossuary under the crypt of St Cecilia. Hence the itineraries mention the numerous saints, ranging in number from seven hundred to eight hundred, buried at this site.

In this activity Damasus, Bishop of Rome, took a leading part. His election, as we have seen, was a disputed one, and the ensuing riots did nothing to enhance the reputation of Christianity in general, or of the successful aspirant in particular. The opponents of Damasus, who had lost possession of the churches, and whose clerical supporters went over to the enemy, held celebrations in honour of the martyrs, without clergy, throughout the cemeteries. At Sant'Agnese, Damasus is alleged to have attacked them with great violence and thus they could represent themselves as the persecuted party, and it is possible that their attitude, parallel to that of the contemporary Donatist schismatics in Africa, would encourage Damasus himself to show the admiration for the martyrs revealed in his search for the location of martyr tombs, and in the verses with which he adorned these, chiselled in the beautiful Filocalian lettering. In his inscription for Peter and Marcellinus, Damasus relates that when he was a boy, the actual executioner of these martyrs told him he had executed them in an unfrequented spot where their sepulchre would never be found, but that Lucilla, a Christian lady, by a revelation from the martyrs themselves, had transferred their bodies. Yet Damasus deprecated burial for himself among the martyrs, saying that he feared to disturb the ashes of the faithful.[11]

The fourth century was, therefore, the great period of the catacombs. Fresh ones were still being dug, such as that near the Via Latina discovered in 1955 during the construction of new

22 (*opposite, right*) The martyrdom of Crispin, Crispinian and Benedicta, from the house under the Church of SS. John and Paul at Rome

23 Fragment of an inscription from the cemetery of Calepodius at Rome, which may indicate commemoration of Callistus as a martyr (YRCA)

24

FAMA·REFERT·SANCTOS·DVDVM·RETVLISSE·PARENTES
AGNEN·CVM·LVGVBRES·CANTVS·TVBA·CONCREPVISSET
NVTRICIS·GREMIVM·SVBITO·LIQVISSE·PVELLAM
SPONTE·TRVCIS·CALCASSE·MINAS·RABIEMQ·TYRANNI
VRERE·CVM·FLAMMIS·VOLVISSET·NOBILE·CORPVS
VIRIB·IN·MENSVM·PARVIS·SVPERASSET·TIMOREM
NVDAQVE·PROFVSVM·CRINEM·PER·MEMBRA·DEDISSE
NE·DOMINI·TEMPLVM·FACIES·PERITVRA·VIDERET
O·VENERANDA·MIHI·SANCTVM·DECVS·ALMA·PVDORIS
VT·DAMASI·PRECIBVS·FAVEAS·PRECOR·INCLYTA·MARTYR

24 Filocalian lettering.
The inscription of
Damasus for St Agnes

buildings. This catacomb is completely self-contained, at a site where the existence of a catacomb had never been suspected. In it were buried about 400 persons. It has no connexion with any martyr. It has yielded a notable number of paintings on subjects hitherto unknown in catacomb art. Its date would seem to be around the middle of the fourth century, and its development extended over a comparatively short period. It probably belonged to a restricted number of wealthy families, and the occurrence among the paintings of scenes from pagan myths may indicate that Christians and pagans were buried together, or that the Christianity of some Christians was penetrated by ideas derived from their pagan past. The date of this catacomb is probably between AD 320 and 360. Some of the *cubicula* have not been fully utilized and one not at all.

But the days of subterranean cemeteries were numbered: the vast labour of deep excavation, the growing insecurity of life and property under barbarian pressure, and a decrease of population all curtailed the use of the catacombs and led to surface graves being used instead. When bishops of Rome were buried at the site of cemeteries the reference is to tombs in churches or above ground. Moreover, the building of basilicas, like that of Peter and Marcellinus, or the *Basilica Apostolorum*, led the faithful to seek tombs in and around these churches. This may account for the number of projected but uncompleted tombs in the catacomb at the site where the former stands.

The cemetery churches, both those already mentioned, and similar ones at Sant' Agnese and St Laurence (*basilica maior*) were built on the same plan, with a nave, and aisles that were extended to form an ambulatory round the apse. 'All the structures in question were densely paved with tombs.'[12] The building of these churches and their ancillary buildings changed the appearance of the countryside around Rome. In the region of the Via Appia and Via Ardeatina there were at least ten such

20

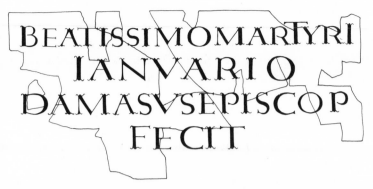

BEATISSIMOMARTYRI
IANVARIO
DAMASVSEPISCOP
FECIT

churches in a circuit of little more than a mile, and in total more than forty in the vicinity of the city. Most of these churches were probably completed by about AD 500. Monasteries were also established at various sites, and probably hostels for the use of pilgrims. We find that a presbyter Barbazion lived in a *cellula*, presumably above ground, at the cemetery of Callistus early in the fifth century. When Boniface I in 418 was engaged in his struggle with Eulalius for the bishopric, he took up his abode at the cemetery of St Felicitas on the Via Salaria Nuova. That implies the existence of a complex of buildings, and the same applies to the prolonged residence of John III (561–74) at the cemetery of Praetextatus.

It is not clear how much damage was done to cemeteries when Rome was captured by the barbarians in AD 410 and 454. But subsequent invasions brought wide-spread destruction; in 537–8 'churches, and bodies of holy martyrs were desecrated by the Goths'. Silverius, pope at this time, was suspected of wishing to surrender the city, perhaps with the object of mitigating such outrages. This desecration particularly applied to the cemeteries of the two Viae Salariae from the direction of which the Goths approached the city. Inscriptions set up by Damasus were destroyed and were replaced; for example, the inscription in honour of Pope Eusebius (d. 310) was re-copied at this period on the reverse of a slab that had previously been used for a dedication to Caracalla, and in the catacomb of Calepodius there has been found a fragment of a pseudo-Damasine inscription in honour of Callistus, which may reflect the restoration of an original after one of the periods of destruction. This is the only inscription of this kind yet found on the Via Aurelia. A similar situation of destruction and restoration ensued at and after the attack by Totila (545–6). We find that John III (561–74) loved and restored the cemeteries of the blessed martyrs and ordered that masses should be celebrated on every Lord's Day by clergy

25 *Praetextatus.*
Inscription set up by Damasus, in memory of Januarius, perhaps one of the deacons of Sixtus II, martyrs in 258

23

from the Lateran, which was then the residence of the popes. This shows that the cemetery churches had no regular clergy of their own, and we can see this also from the account of Sergius I (687–701), who, as a presbyter attached to the church of St Susanna, had been indefatigable in celebrating mass throughout the various cemeteries. Gregory III (731–41) ordered that vigils and masses should take place in the cemeteries round Rome on the feast days of the various saints, through clergy he himself had appointed.

It was natural that efforts should be made to keep in use the large basilicas built throughout the cemeteries. One stage in their use was the transference of the relics of martyrs from catacombs to churches. We shall shortly come to a consideration of the itineraries produced for the use of pilgrims, but here it may be stated that visitors saw the graves of many martyrs in the cemetery churches. The last systematic efforts to renew and repair the churches and the cemeteries themselves were made in the long pontificates of Hadrian I (772–95) and Leo III (795–816). The activities of these two popes were wide-spread, but the final abandonment of the suburban cemeteries was at hand. In the insecurity which prevailed for centuries the countryside around Rome became desert, and the relics were transferred not to cemetery churches but to churches located *inside the city*.

This process was not one that began suddenly. In the late fourth century, for example, Ambrose of Milan regarded it as most appropriate, that where the Redeemer was the victim *on* the altar those whom he had redeemed should lie under it (cf. Rev. 6.9). But as far as the catacombs are concerned, decisive points are the transference of 28 wagon-loads of relics to the Pantheon, consecrated as S. Maria ad martyres, in 609, when the structure was given to Boniface IV by the Byzantine emperor Phocas. But some authorities question the extent of this transference.[13]

It was under Paul I (757–67) that transference on a large scale followed the Lombard invasion of 756, when the invaders did great damage to cemeteries, and even carried off the bodies of martyrs. Paul found the catacombs and their churches in a sorry state. The honours shown to martyrs at their tombs had come near to ceasing. Animals wandered freely, and were even stabled, in the cemeteries. Such a situation moved the Pope to bring, with due ceremony, the relics of martyrs, confessors and virgins into the city, and establish there a monastery, the members of which could pay to the martyrs the honour due to them. As we have

26 *Pamphilus*. An altar (sixth century) for the celebration of Mass at the tomb of a martyr, with a repository for relics in its lower part

already seen, Hadrian I and Leo III made vigorous efforts to preserve the cemeteries, but their efforts could do little beyond touching the fringe of a vast problem. Paschal I (817–24), Leo's successor, found the crypts of the martyrs destroyed and abandoned, and on 20 July 817 he had the bodies of 2,300 martyrs transferred to the church of S. Prassede. Sergius II (844–7) and Leo IV (847–55) pursued the quest for relics of illustrious martyrs 'lying in the ruined cemeteries', but by their time the potentiality of the catacombs as a source for genuine relics was largely exhausted.

The relics of various martyrs, even some of the most illustrious ones, were however destined to find their resting place far from Rome. The rapid spread of Christianity in countries north of the Alps led to an almost insatiable desire for relics to enhance the popularity of recently founded churches and abbeys. Rome had become a centre for pilgrimage, but the multitudes who could not visit Rome desired to have in their own countries relics of the saints of earlier centuries. Rome was the great storehouse of relics. If emperors sought these, the demand was hard to refuse, but sometimes the Romans resisted the spoliation of martyrs' tombs. At the beginning of the sixth century, Gregory the Great resisted a request from the empress Constantina for relics of St Paul, 'his head or some other part of his body', for a church in the palace at Constantinople. The Pope replied that it was not a Roman custom to touch any part of a saint's body. The surrender of St Sebastian to Soissons required long and anxious deliberation on the part of Pope Eugenius II (824–7) and his advisers, and that of Alexander, reputed fifth bishop of Rome after Peter but probably a martyr of later date, at whose tomb miracles of healing took place, provoked popular resistance.

There were those to whom trade in relics proved lucrative, and as a type of these one may take the Roman deacon Deusdona (early ninth century). He lived near the church of St Peter ad Vincula, and possibly was in charge (in so far as this was still apposite) of the catacomb of SS. Peter and Marcellinus, of which he showed, in dealing with clients, complete and perfect knowledge. Thither he guided emissaries in search of relics, and thence was extracted a rich haul, including the two above-mentioned saints, and their fellow martyr Tiburtius. But Deusdona did not merely wait at Rome for customers. He made several journeys to the North to promote business, where he whetted the appetites of his hosts by a skilful combination of reluctance on the one hand, and hints of what he could supply on the other. He even seems to have carried a prospectus of what was available, and specimens in his luggage! Thus the Northern abbeys, Fulda in particular, were richly endowed with relics of the Roman martyrs, and we may infer that Deusdona was also richly endowed, but in a purely material sense. The relics were not all genuine. For a thousand years those of St Hyacinthus were believed to be at Seligenstadt, but his tomb was found, intact, in the cemetery of Hermes in 1845.

The ninth century begins the period of oblivion. We must now consider visitors to the catacombs, those of the centuries of pilgrimage, those of the centuries of neglect, and those by whose efforts the catacombs have again been revealed to the world.

27 Inscription of St Hyacinthus, found in the catacomb of Hermes at Rome in 1845

D P. III · IDVS · SEBI EBRO

YACINTHVS
MARTYR

3

The Rediscovery of the Catacombs

Questa misteriosa città de secoli eroici del cristianesimo . . .

G. B. de Rossi, Preface to *Roma Sotterranea*

According to the *Liber Pontificalis*, Cornelius, Bishop of Rome from 251 to 253, was buried by the matron Lucina in a crypt near the cemetery of Callistus on the Appian Way, on her own property, and not in the Papal Crypt. In 1848 G. B. de Rossi found, near this cemetery, part of an inscription containing the words . . . NELIUS MARTYR, and in 1852, as he pursued his investigations, the other part of the stone was found *in situ*, and the tomb of Cornelius was thus discovered.[14] A shrine of considerable size had been built over his tomb by Leo I in the fifth century, but this building had disappeared long ago.

In investigating the catacombs, de Rossi had studied any documents that gave topographical indications, such as the *Liber Pontificalis*, martyrologies and various itineraries compiled for the use of pilgrims. These documents proved their value on numerous occasions, and the use of the material contained in them took away haphazard elements in the investigation of the catacombs, from which earlier investigators suffered.

In the Filocalian Calendar of 354 dates are given month by month for the annual celebration of festivals of martyrs at Rome. Besides martyrs buried in catacombs, there are included the Apostles Peter and Paul, the Africans Perpetua and Felicitas, and Cyprian. The last-named was celebrated on 14 September, in the catacomb of Callistus, perhaps at the tomb of his contemporary Cornelius, with whose episcopate his own had historically been so closely linked, and at which, about the sixth century, pictures were placed of Cornelius and Cyprian, and of Sixtus II and Optatus (a Mauretanian bishop whose relics were brought to Rome about that period). Later on it was believed that Cyprian was actually buried in this catacomb!

The *Itineraries* were compiled between the seventh and the twelfth centuries. These were particularly directed to the needs of pilgrims. But before considering the *Itineraries*, it may be well to mention briefly the activities of an emissary named John, who carried oil from the lamps that burned at the shrines of martyrs to Theodelinda, Queen of the Lombards, in the time of Gregory the Great (end of sixth century). An index to the shrines visited, some of the bottles that contained the oil, and a number of the labels attached to these bottles are preserved in the cathedral at Monza. From these pieces of evidence we can deduce that John, or whoever actually collected the oil, did not visit the shrines in a systematic manner: some of the roads, on which shrines existed, are entirely omitted. It is clear that the number of saints was being multiplied – and by implication the number of martyrs. On the Via Appia, the two Viae Salariae and the Via Nomentana there are references to 'thousands of saints'. But in the time of Gregory the exportation of relics had not begun.

The *Itineraries*, designed to guide the pilgrim through Christian Rome, were not a new literary form. Once pilgrimages to an area began, guides were necessary. Examples of these are the *Itinerary from Bordeaux to Jerusalem*, written in 333, soon after such journeys had begun on a large scale in the time of Constantine, or the *Pilgrimage of Egeria* from Gaul to the sacred sites of the East, written about the end of the fourth century. The Roman *Itineraries* begin in the seventh century with *Notitia ecclesiarum urbis Romae*, composed under Pope Honorius I, and *De locis sanctis martyrum quae sunt foris civitatis Romae* is of about the same date.

The method followed in the *Itineraries* was to go round the roads which radiate from Rome. They circulated either in a clockwise or anti-clockwise direction, a method that can be, and still is followed in dealing with the catacombs. They were probably written in Rome, and copies were secured by Christians who wished to visit the sacred sites. While they appear to be rather dull and lifeless, their importance – and accuracy – was proved, as has already been mentioned, when the scientific rediscovery of the catacombs began in the nineteenth century. On one occasion even the number of steps that one must descend is mentioned.

For English-speaking readers it is interesting to note that one *Itinerary* occurs in the work of William of Malmesbury, *De Gestis Regum Anglorum* (twelfth century), perhaps intended for the use of Crusaders. But the topographical indications contained in it are not of the twelfth century, because included are catacombs that were inaccessible by that date and martyr tombs from which the relics had been removed.

The *Itineraries* may be dated to before the year 1100. Thereafter, for several centuries, we know nothing about the catacombs. Any visitors must have been casual ones, seekers after (supposed) buried treasure, or marble that could be reduced to lime. As sanctuaries of Christian devotion they were forgotten, and the cemetery churches must generally have become ruinous. While access to St Sebastian was always possible, even the names of most individual cemeteries had disappeared. When, for example, Onofrius Panvinius produced, in 1568, his *De ritu sepeliendi mortuos apud veteres Christianos et de eorundem coemeteriis*, he identified three cemeteries only by name, those of St Sebastian, St Ciriaca (at the church of St Laurence), and St Valentine (on the Via Flaminia). Confusion about the names of cemeteries persisted down to the nineteenth century. Thus we read: 'Those catacombs [of St Sebastian, but believed to be those of St Callistus] are supposed to have an extension of six miles. It is stated by ecclesiastical writers that 14 popes and 170,000 martyrs were buried within them.'[15]

In a *cubiculum* of the cemetery of Callistus there is found the name JOHANNES LONCK with the date 1432. The same catacomb was visited on 8 June 1433 by some *fratres minores*, and members of this order continued to go there at various dates in the fifteenth century, including one visit 'in the week in which Pope Nicholas V died' (in 1455); on 19 May 1469 an abbot of St Sebastian came, with many others, and in 1467 'some Scots were here'. But these visits imply no more than what De Rossi called 'pious curiosity'.

Towards the end of the fifteenth century, however, we meet with the earliest explorers. These were members of the Roman Academy. They have left their names in Peter and Marcellinus, in Praetextatus, and in Callistus, and in their impromptu inscriptions refer to themselves as UNANIMES ANTIQUITATIS AMATORES or PERSCRUTATORES ANTIQUITATIS. Their leader Pomponius Letus and his friends were accused of being pagans, and of conspiracy against the Pope. In an inscription of 1475 occur the words REGNANTE POM. PONT. MAX., and in another, POMPONIUS PONT. MAX., while yet another visitor is called SACERDOS ACADEMIAE ROM. When the members of the Academy were brought to trial, these inscriptions were not known: they may not, of course, amount to more than academic pleasantries. No record exists of any discovery, say of inscriptions, having been made on these visits. But an impulse to visit catacombs had now been given. By the end of the fifteenth century the graves of martyrs and other early Christians under the basilica of San Pancrazio on the Via Aurelia were being visited. 'The bodies can be seen and touched, but on no account are they to be removed, under threat of papal excommunication, unless under a special licence granted by the Pope.' Such visits may, however, have led to the virtual ruination of this catacomb.

Both St Charles Borromeo (1538–84) and St Philip Neri (1515–95) visited the catacomb of St Sebastian for prayer and meditation. But it was in 1578 that lively interest was aroused when diggers of *pozzolana* lighted on a catacomb on the Via Salaria Nuova. Baronius (1538–1601) has described the excitement caused in Rome by this event: 'Wonderful to relate, we saw, and often walked in the cemetery of Priscilla [it was really the catacomb of the Jordani], not long ago found and excavated on the Via Salaria at the third milestone from the city. We can find no better expression to describe it, and its many different passages than "a city beneath the earth". Rome was astonished when she knew that she had, in her vicinity, Christian communities, once Christian colonies in time of persecution, but now filled only with tombs. There arose a fuller understanding of what was written in literary works, or was seen from other cemeteries only partly revealed. What she had read in St Jerome or Prudentius, she saw with her own eyes, and beheld things such as to excite lively wonder.'

While this discovery itself was not followed up, the time was at hand for a general revival of interest in the catacombs. In the latter years of the century Alphonso Chacon (Ciacconio), Philip de Winghe (d. 1592) and Jean L'Heureux (Macarius) copied the pictures accessible to them. Ciacconio employed six copyists. They used the style with which they were familiar and not the style of the pictures that they were copying. The first copyist, who copied frescoes, now lost, from the cemetery of the Jordani 'was not able to divest his subjects of the attitudes employed in classical sculpture'. From the catacomb of Novella came a 'good 28 shepherd' transformed into a girl in a farmyard; it was described by Ciacconio as St Priscilla herself feeding the preachers of the gospel, represented as cocks, and the faithful Christians 29 represented as sheep. Most remarkable of all is Noah in the Ark, who is described as 'St Marcellus, Pope and martyr, inspired in

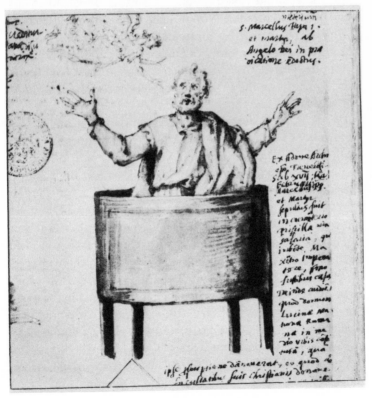

28 The work of St Priscilla. One of Ciacconio's copyists has transformed a Good Shepherd into a girl in a farmyard (St Priscilla)

29 One of Ciacconio's copyists has transformed Noah in the ark (cf. Ill. 42) into Pope Marcellus (308–9) preaching

preaching by an angel of God'. Noah appears to have attracted misconceptions. Ciacconio's fourth copyist turned him into a deacon, clad in the usual diaconal 'dalmatic', with similar angelic inspiration vouchsafed to him. De Winghe saw that Ciacconio's pictures were inaccurate, but died in 1592 before he could publish his corrections.

But the first great explorer of the catacombs was Antonio Bosio (c. 1576–1629), perhaps a Maltese by birth, who inherited from an uncle the office of agent of the Knights of Malta in Rome. His first expeditions took place in 1593, when he must have been under twenty years of age; in his book *Roma Sotterranea* one finds mention, with dates, of his constant visits to the catacombs. His work was not published till after his death. The learning and tenacity shown by Bosio are outstanding. His book begins with the Vatican cemetery and proceeds round Rome, anti-clockwise, till he reaches the Via Flaminia. He does not mention any *Itinerary* except that of William of Malmesbury. His method was to go out searching for entrances, often with little success. 'I have many times', he writes, 'gone out from the Porta Portuensis and searched the country round, and made enquiries from old vinedressers, but between 1600 and 1618 I found only two entrances.' But in all he found entrances to about thirty cemeteries, whereas his immediate predecessor Ciacconio had visited some five only. Sometimes his entrances were, as might be expected, through *lucernaria*. On 7 August 1601 he got into a cemetery on the Via Nomentana by one of these, with the help of a ladder and ropes.

Bosio's work is far more than a mere account of his own discoveries. He began by considering the whole question of the death and burial of the martyrs, whose numbers he took to be very great, 'l'infinito numero de Martiri'; to take an example, four thousand martyrs were killed under Hadrian on the Via Appia! Before he considers the cemeteries of each road, he gives a history of the road itself, derived from classical and later authors, of the martyrs associated with it, and finally of his own discoveries. He did not explore all the cemeteries where martyrs are buried. Over and over again he speaks of passages filled with earth, and during his long life he did not make anything that one can call an excavation; he studied hardly anything but unencumbered and accessible passages.[16] He was hindered by lack of funds. He comments, correctly, on the height of passages in Peter and Marcellinus and the lowness of passages in Cyriaca, and how one catacomb had been joined to another.

Bosio illustrated his work with representations of the catacomb paintings. He employed two collaborators whose efforts were not always accurate. The signatures of the principal one, Toccafondo, and of Bosio himself are in the catacomb of St Soter (part of Callistus): IO ANGELUS TOCCAFUNDUS PINXIT DIE 18 JUNII 1596 ANT. BOSIUS FECIT. But in general one can deduce from *Roma Sotterranea* a very fair impression of the subjects represented in catacomb art. The reproductions by Ciacconio and De Winghe were in part used by Bosio for pictures from the cemetery of the Jordani, discovered, as has been stated, in 1578, but destroyed by diggers of *pozzolana* before Bosio wrote. He adds, 'They did not go unpunished; after doing this damage, so big a landslide took place that they were overwhelmed.' This catacomb was rediscovered only in 1921.

The fourth and last book of *Roma Sotterranea* was the work of his editor Severanus, who had at his disposal many notes made by Bosio and who left the whole work under Bosio's name. The general subject of this book is the question of the meaning that should be attributed to the catacomb paintings. Severanus is particularly anxious to show that the Christian burial places were not contaminated by pagans, heretics or schismatics, that signs and symbols used by pagans were taken over by Christians but had gained new significations. The work of Bosio stimulated interest in the catacombs: during the seventeenth century there was a succession of visitors and explorers. The search for relics was resumed as men became alerted to the number of supposed martyrs buried there. Misson, in his *New Voyage to Italy* (1688), remarks, 'consequently, which is the cream of the story, ... they [the catacombs] are an inexhaustible storehouse of relics'.[17] Detractors of Bosio were not wanting, and it was put about that in his (supposed) explorations the catacombs were the scene of drunken orgies.

Misson, and Bishop Burnet (who visited Italy in 1685–6) are quite sceptical about the Christian nature of the catacombs. Both authors comment on the catacombs at Naples and at Rome. Misson regarded them as common burial places of all – in fact *puticoli* – and that Christian symbols were used merely to distinguish Christian from heathen tombs, and that they belong principally to the fourth and fifth centuries. Burnet shared this opinion, but was even more sceptical about the antiquity of inscriptions and paintings – 'the manner and characters are Gothick'. He observed the catacombs carefully, both at Rome and at Naples ('to which the catacombs at Rome are not to be compared'), and at the latter the (apparent) absence of stones or tiles to cover the tombs made him think that bodies were laid in them without covering: 'It seems that they were monstrous, unwholesome and stinking places, where some thousands of bodies lay rotting, without anything to shut in so loathsome a sight, and so odious a smell.' Notwithstanding his interest Burnet did not like catacombs: 'I began to grow weary of the darkness and the thick air of the place, so that I staid not above an hour in the catacombs.' Both Misson and Burnet simply refused to believe that there were enough Christians to dig the catacombs: Burnet was particularly sceptical about the number of Christians at Naples. Such criticisms existed also in other countries, e.g. Germany, and de Rossi comments most severely on the work in this vein of Peter Zorn, professor at Hamburg: 'the tares once sown took root – the professor of Hamburg moves me to laughter, who from Leipzig (his place of publication) wished to teach Bosio himself what catacombs are!'

The plundering of the catacombs in order to obtain 'relics' led to widespread destruction, as the relic hunters were not interested in antiquities or history. In 1672 Clement X established the office of 'Guardian of the Sacred Relics and of the Cemeteries', but this appointment was not effective in stopping depredation and destruction. Early holders of this office included Fabretti (1618–1700), who recommended the exploration of the catacombs, and began to study the inscriptions with some sort of scientific method; Boldetti (1663–1749) who was 'Guardian' for over thirty years; and Marangoni (1673–1753), Boldetti's friend and collaborator for more than twenty years. Boldetti was utterly unsystematic in his removal of objects from the cemeteries, but his *Observations* published in 1720 have an interest in their reference to material accessible to him over a long period of years, and now lost. The work was undertaken at the request of Clement to counter the objections raised – and that not by Protestants only – against the excessive veneration of martyrs and relics. Boldetti's work was vitiated by lack of order, bad description and inexact quotation. When de Rossi came to publish his *Inscriptiones Christianae urbis Romae* (I, 1857–61) he castigated Boldetti for his errors and his *ignava incuria*.

Marangoni continued Boldetti's work, with greater attention to arrangement and accurate description, but his records were in great measure destroyed in a fire in 1737. Criticism of the random dispersal of inscriptions led Boldetti and Marangoni to approach the Pope with a proposal to form a collection of inscriptions at the Vatican. But eventually these were transferred to various churches in Rome.

Clement XII committed to G. G. Bottari (1689–1775) the task of reissuing the work of Bosio. But apart from identity of title, i.e. *Roma Sotterranea*, the work is not a reissue of Bosio, which Bottari considered inferior to the volume edited by Severanus. Bottari produced a commentary on the pictures published by Bosio, but he neglected completely personal investigation of the catacombs, and his commentary on the monuments follows *un parfait désordre*.[18] Discoveries made since Bosio's day were not treated – this would have been a hard enough task, in view of the methods of his immediate predecessors – with the exception of the catacomb of Vibia, which Bottari mentions[19] as not yet having been published.

Not only were inscriptions and sculpture removed from the catacombs, but efforts were made to remove pictures as well. Boldetti tried to do so, and Seroux d'Agincourt (1730–1814) attempted it on a larger scale. The results were disastrous: 'No one can say how much useless destruction was carried out in the name of a false love of antiquity.'[20]

It was not until the nineteenth century that exploration of the catacombs was carried out in a scientific manner, particularly by G. Settele (1770–1840), and G. Marchi (1795–1860). These were the immediate predecessors of G. B. de Rossi (1822–94) whose work, extending over nearly fifty years, was monumental both in its discoveries, and in the foundations it laid for all subsequent investigators. He had the support of Marchi, of Pope Pius IX, and of his brother M. S. de Rossi. His *Roma Sotterranea* appeared in 1864 and the following years, and was translated or adapted into English, French and German.

From the late nineteenth century on, investigations and discoveries in other areas besides Rome and its vicinity have been wide-spread. In particular one may mention Naples, Sicily in general, Malta and Tunisia as the scenes of such discoveries. The work is never-ending; new catacombs are still being found, new regions in existing ones are being opened up, and out of the insights so gained new light is thrown on the thought, worship and practices of the early Christians.

The Decoration of the Catacombs

The catacomb paintings perpetuate, celebrate, confirm the anonymous faith of those ages and people.

E. R. Goodenough.[21]

Pictures in the catacombs and reliefs on sarcophagi are almost the sole remaining forms of Christian art that survive from the centuries of persecution. The discovery of the baptistery/church at Dura Europos in Mesopotamia has proved that pictures were also placed on the walls of such buildings. The paintings at Dura are anterior to the destruction of the city in AD 256. That paintings might be placed in churches, even in distant provinces of the West, is clear from canon 37 of the Council of Elvira in Spain, held in the early fourth century, whatever the precise meaning of the wording of the canon may be: 'There shall be no pictures in church, lest what is reverenced and adored be depicted on the walls.' But these early church buildings have perished. The destruction of such buildings was one of the methods employed in the great persecution of 303–11, and this may account, in no small measure, for their disappearance. Lactantius tells us of the destruction of the church at Nicomedia, a building of considerable prominence in the city, and even Constantius I, the father of Constantine, who alone of the emperors of that time did not sympathize with the policy of persecution, destroyed a few churches as a token of solidarity with his more intransigent colleagues.

Common circumstances of life compelled Christians to possess and use objects bearing artistic representations. Emblems on seals were universal. Clement of Alexandria[22] points out that certain of these were particularly suitable for Christians, for example, a dove, a fish, a ship, a lyre; several of them become symbols common in catacomb art. But we must not imagine that Christians specifically ordered such emblems from the makers. They were already in use in circumstances that had nothing to do with Christianity.

Moreover, Tertullian tells us that Christians used drinking cups – probably the 'gold-glass' vessels of which so many fragments are found – carrying representations of a 'good shepherd' bearing a sheep on his shoulders. As we shall see, these need not be representations of the Christian Good Shepherd, nor does Tertullian regard them as such; with a sidelong glance at the *Shepherd of Hermas*, a work which permitted one more chance to sinners after baptism who later repented, Tertullian regards the shepherd on these cups as the patron of drunkenness and adultery, who was willing to forgive those who had committed sins commonly regarded as unforgivable.

In the early centuries the connexion between art and paganism was blazoned forth everywhere. This was particularly obvious in cities where magnificent temples and statues, devoted to the glory of the gods, could attract or repel the viewer. Towards these artistic representations Christians could only feel repugnance. The gods were malignant demons, and escape from their power was one of the things that Christianity promised. There was the explicit prohibition in scripture, in the Book of Exodus, of the making or worshipping of images. That prohibition should apply to Jews even more than to Christians, but among the former we find that there had never been strict observance of this precept, as is evident from the Old Testament descriptions of Solomon's temple and throne. But in the course of centuries its validity had to some extent become eroded. The most obvious example of this is in the decoration of the synagogue at Dura, where not only was mural decoration involving human figures freely used, but actual scenes from the Old Testament were represented. It is possible that the congregation of this synagogue was not a strictly orthodox one. At Rome, meanwhile, Jewish *fossores* were tunnelling diligently at the same time as their Christian counterparts, and from *their* catacombs decoration was not absent, even human figures being represented, though no scenes from the Old Testament have yet been discovered. 'There was manifestly no scruple, at least among the less conservative members, about the use of human and animal figures in their decorations', and moreover 'some of the paintings are evidently the work of artists of no mean skill.'[23] It is evident, then, that syncretism or the influence of proselytes had abrogated strict religious principles for some Jews.

The decoration of tombs by paintings had a long history, and did not originate with Jews or Christians. Quite apart from the famous Etruscan paintings at Cerveteri or Tarquinia, examples

31

31 Jewish catacomb at Rome. Decoration of ceiling

may be seen at Rome in *columbaria* (buildings with niches for holding urns containing ashes) such as that of Pomponius Hylas near the Porta Latina, or those in the same area contiguous to the catacomb adjoining the tombs of the Scipios. Perhaps the best example of pagan tomb painting found at Rome was at the Tomb of the Statilii near the Porta Maggiore, excavated in 1875. A small adjacent tomb contained a painted frieze of the time of Augustus, with illustrations from Vergil's *Aeneid* and the early history of Rome. The vaulted ceiling, now no longer accessible, contained paintings of the third century similar in form, if not in subject, to contemporary paintings in the catacombs – Fortune with a cornucopia, Apollo and a female figure, Hercules and a female figure, Hippolytus and Phaedra; there is also a scene with a sepulcral banquet of a type found frequently in Christian tombs.[24] The decoration of pagan tombs shows, in general, walls with painted architectural features, garlands of leaves or foliage, vines with bunches of grapes, peacocks, doves and other birds, sea creatures and *genii*.

It has already been mentioned that, on our available evidence, nothing is known about the painters of the catacombs; whether at the earliest stage they were Christians or not, or whether painters and *fossores* were the same people. It is clear however that they were simply following pagan predecessors. 'The art of late antiquity was a large family, to which the first Christian art belonged.'[25] A considerable part of the surviving painting has nothing, or very little, to do with Christianity. Leaving aside the painting of mere patterns of different colours, we find, for example, a large area of the so-called Crypt of the Flavians in the catacomb of Domitilla decorated with flowers and foliage; from this it is only a step, so to speak, to a light well in the catacomb of
6 Praetextatus, where there is not only similar decoration but also *putti* harvesting, or to representations of Cupid and Psyche gathering flowers. Heads representing the seasons are also commonly portrayed, as are sea creatures such as sea-horses. A great deal of this kind of painting may be said to reflect a general preoccupation with annual cycles of recurring life and death, which occupied no small place in the religious thought of the ancient world: the 'Christian' painters took over themes with which they were already familiar, and these themes were not considered inappropriate by those who commissioned the paintings and by those who were in charge of the catacombs.

We have no means of telling at what stage of construction or of use a *cubiculum* received its decoration. The ceilings, on which so

GORGONIVS

many of the paintings occur, could be decorated as soon as the chamber was hollowed out, but the process of filling a *cubiculum* with graves must in some cases have extended over a lengthy period. In the case of a *cubiculum* in St Callistus, we find that the plastering was done in a single process, and so the whole chamber may have received painting likewise: we find also, quite frequently, evidence of paintings being broken to admit of the hollowing-out of a new *loculus*.

The era of catacomb painting began about AD 200 or soon after, and came to an end in the fifth century when burials ceased. After that date pictures were still placed in catacombs in subterranean basilicas, to which the faithful resorted, or at other spots of particular sanctity. These are generally pictures of martyrs or saints, sometimes those buried in the catacomb concerned; or of Apostles, of the Virgin, or of our Lord himself. An 'early' example of this kind is seen on the ceiling of a *cubiculum* in the catacomb of Peter and Marcellinus where Christ

32 *Peter and Marcellinus.* Christ enthroned, between SS. Peter and Paul. Early fifth century (?)

32 appears in glory with the Apostles Peter and Paul, while below are the four martyrs with whom this catacomb was associated, Peter, Marcellinus, Gorgonius and Tiburtius. Between them stands the Lamb, as in the Book of Revelation (14.1), on the holy mountain of Zion from which flow the four rivers of Paradise. Such a delineation may be based on a picture or mosaic in a church. Other examples of this type of art are the pictures, already mentioned, of Cornelius and Cyprian at the tomb of the former, and the pictures of various saints in the catacombs of Pontian and Commodilla. These late pictures, in their statuesque delineation of the figures, are Byzantine in type, and may easily be distinguished from pictures dating from the centuries when the catacombs were in use.

The cost of decoration must generally have been borne by the more well-to-do Christians, and the social status of Christians buried in this or that part of a cemetery may be estimated from the amount of paintings, or of positions suitable for paintings; for example, the catacomb of the Via Latina contains one gallery only in which there are simple *loculi*; the other burials are in richly ornamental *cubicula*. It is possible that the expense of decorating tombs of martyrs would be borne by Christians in general or by the parishes to which individual catacombs were attached. It has been remarked that 'wealthier Christians do not seem to have been quite so ready to spend money on the tombs of the martyrs as on their own family vaults.'[26]

The Christians sometimes used sarcophagi for burials. These were principally placed in *cubicula*. The relief sculptures with which they were decorated depict in general the same subjects as the paintings. The two arts grew up together: initially the Christians bought their sarcophagi from the same shop as the pagans, and then added, or did not add, specifically Christian decoration. Simpler than the art of the sarcophagi are reliefs or paintings on actual *loculi*. We find these in both Jewish and Christian catacombs, and in style they vary from careful creation

33 to mere *graffiti*. In Jewish catacombs are representations of the
34 *menorah* (seven-branched candlestick), of the *lulab* (branch or twig), of the *etrog* (fruit) and of the *shofar* (horn). These signs, alone or in combination, may mean nothing more than an indication that the tomb is Jewish. But there was no need to emphasize this in a cemetery devoted entirely to Jewish burials. Christian signs on *their* tombs are the leaf, the tree, and those of more specific Christian import, such as the fish, the dove or the anchor. Perhaps we can best regard these as a sign of feeling for

the dead – their tombs should not be left by relatives and friends without some token. But on questions of feeling we must be cautious, because the greater number of *loculi*, both Jewish and Christian, are without marks or inscriptions of any kind. It did not seem ultimately to matter.

33 Jewish tomb, inscription of Delphinus, a ruler

When we pass on to consider actual inscriptions, the wording of both Jewish and Christian examples is usually utterly simple. The most notable feature of both, which distinguishes them from all other sepulchral inscriptions, is the frequent reference to PEACE: EN EIRENE(I) HE KOIMESIS SOU – in peace thy sleep – say the Greek inscriptions on Jewish graves; Christian ones say more often simply IN PACE but references to sleeping are also found. Both Jews and Christians are referring to Psalm 4.8, 'In peace . . . I shall sleep', or possibly, but appositely in the case of martyrs, to the Book of Wisdom 3.3, 'But they are in peace', (after affliction), (cf. p. 154). Obvious features of tombstones are, of course, the name and age of the deceased, some reference to family relationships, and to occupation, the date of burial, including sometimes the consular year. There is little theological statement.

34 Jewish tomb, inscription of Judas, a priest

Sometimes there are representations of persons which purport to be likenesses of the deceased. Some of these may be genuine, and there may be real likenesses in some of the often repeated representations of *orantes*, figures with hands raised in the attitude of prayer. The figure of the *orans* had a long past in pagan art before it was adopted by the Christians. Among the latter its use was universal, in Rome, Syracuse, Naples and North Africa. As examples of possible portraits one may cite the *orant* in the catacomb of Priscilla called *Donna velata*, the picture of a young woman in the catacomb of Thrason, or of Dionysias in the catacomb of Callistus, or of a man in the hunting scenes in the *hypogaeum* of 'the hunters' on the Via Appia Antica. On sarcophagi we can see portraits on the medallions, frequently of husband and wife, which occur on one of the longer sides, e.g. on the sarcophagus (to be dated *c.* 350) of Adelfia, wife of Count Valerius, found in the catacomb of San Giovanni at Syracuse, and now in the National Museum there. It is impossible to regard pictures of Christ, of Apostles, of biblical characters, or of martyrs, as having any genuine resemblance to the persons represented. The Carpocratians, heretics of the second century, were supposed by Irenaeus to have images and/or pictures of Christ, made by Pilate (!), and of various philosophers. But these, if they existed, could not have had any authority among

63

35

35 Syracuse. San
Giovanni. The
sarcophagus of Adelfia,
wife of Count Valerius

Catholic Christians. In any case there was no fixed idea in Christian art of Christ's appearance; sometimes he is bearded, sometimes not. And it must be noted that the symbolic representation of Christ as the Good Shepherd continues a type that goes far back before the beginning of the Christian era, and many 'good shepherds' are found, particularly on sarcophagi, that have nothing to do with Christianity. Reference has already been made to representations of a 'shepherd' on 'gold-glass' vessels (page 56, above).

No attempt will be made in this book to assign dates to the catacomb pictures or decoration except in certain cases where the position, subject or style of the paintings enables a judgement to be made. We shall, rather, proceed to consider what the pictures tell us about the religion of the Christians.

5

The Old Testament and the Catacombs

Whatever was written in former days was written for our instruction, that by steadfastness and by the encouragement of the scriptures we might have hope.

Romans 15.4 R.S.V.

By the time that catacombs became important, i.e. in the middle of the third century, Christianity had evolved its main doctrines. Assuredly much remained to be settled in the Trinitarian and Christological controversies of the fourth and fifth centuries, but the main lines of doctrinal development were already established. This faith was derived from the Holy Scriptures of the Old and New Testaments, from the doctrinal traditions established everywhere with wonderful unanimity among the Churches, and from practices and ideas which, if not expressly sanctioned in scripture, did not contradict it. These were summed up by Tertullian in his dictum that 'tradition was their originator, custom their strengthener and faith their observer'.

Tertullian also remarked that the confidence of Christians rested on the resurrection of the dead: 'by it we are believers'. There is, of course, nothing remarkable in Tertullian's pronouncement. He is merely emphasizing what St Paul had written in I Corinthians, that the death and resurrection of Christ were of first importance (15.3): 'If Christ has not been raised, your faith is futile' (15.17); 'Christ is the first fruits of those who have fallen asleep' (15.20). It was in this confidence that the Christians buried their dead, and we might expect to find illustrated in the catacombs a reflection of this confidence. In this we shall not be disappointed, though we may be surprised at the way in which it is portrayed. For the Passion, Resurrection and Ascension of Christ are not subjects in which the inscriptions and art of the catacombs show any particular interest. And in passing we may note that the most obvious representation of resurrection in the Old Testament, the vision of Ezekiel 37, has not yet been found in Christian art. Its appearance in the synagogue at Dura is another story, and does not concern us here.

The survival of evidence from paintings, inscriptions, reliefs and *graffiti* depends on chances and mischances that it is not possible to elucidate. We should expect, however, that the scenes from the Old Testament, portrayed in the cemeteries, would have a significance appropriate to their use on graves. We shall find this to be the case on a number of occasions. But it is probably right to regard these scenes in the context of the life that Christians led in the world, a life in which danger often threatened and occasionally became an actuality. Hence scenes of peril and deliverance from peril are common. But the Christians were exposed also to danger from unseen foes, the demons, who inspired pagans and persecutors, and a scene of deliverance implied a victory over the demons as well.

However, even when we have taken scenes of this kind into account, there are others for the appearance of which no apparent reason can be given. Such pictures must have corresponded to the personal predilection of those who commissioned them. Old Testament scenes play a large part in the subjects depicted, and the reason for this may be that these scenes were drawn from liturgical usage and from funeral rites, which in turn were drawn from Jewish sources.

The Old Testament was used also by Christians to prefigure 'things to come', and certain pictures could be regarded in this light. But it is probably advisable to be chary of deriving catacomb paintings from references in early Christian literature, because the literary works are often of a later date than the paintings. We shall look therefore first at the material derived from the Old Testament. In subjects the pictures are very diversified, but it is worth noting that the new catacomb of the Via Latina has presented us with pictures from the Old Testament that are new to catacomb decoration as we know it, and those who commissioned these pictures appear to have had a fuller appreciation of the Old Testament story than is elsewhere found. D. Kaufmann, writing in 1887,[27] commented on the absence of certain scenes from the repertoire of catacomb art, which have turned up among the Via Latina pictures. But even so it is difficult always to assign meanings appropriate to death and to deliverance from death. The Via Latina pictures are so wide-ranging in their scope that it will be best to leave them (with a few exceptions) until later, and concentrate on scenes

familiar to investigators of the catacombs before the Via Latina pictures were discovered.

36 Malta: The Creation, perhaps the naming of the animals (Gen. 2. 19–20). From a country catacomb near Gudia

Early Christian art had no inhibitions about representing God: catacomb paintings, and reliefs on sarcophagi portray a figure, of which no other explanation can be given, but we may interpose the query whether such representations are of the Father or of his agent in creation, the *Demiurgus*, or in Catholic parlance, the 'Word, by whom all things were made'. Such a possibility may be apparent in a country catacomb in Malta, where we see the naming of the animals by Adam, those creatures subject to man from the beginning, and once more to be tamed by the Christ-Orpheus, who appears also in catacomb art (p. 101, below). In the *Hypogaeum* of the Viale Manzoni (see pp. 111ff., below), a figure is seen in close juxtaposition to the scenes of Adam, Eve and the serpent, and in the catacomb of the Via Latina, God can be seen expelling Adam and Eve from Eden, and pouring water from heaven to cause the Flood (but see p. 84, below).

36

37

But let us begin with pictures of the Fall, the event which 'brought death into this world and all our woe'. Nowhere is this more appositely shown that at Dura-Europos, where the pictures of the Fall and of the Good Shepherd are side by side in the baptistery.

38

Representations of the Fall are wide-spread both in number and in diversity of locality. They occur in paintings, on sarcophagi and on glass cups, of wide provenance. Other features of the Eden story are not unknown, but are rare, such as the creation of Eve, the naming of the animals (to which reference has already been made) and the expulsion from the Garden.

As the story of humanity unfolds, we may see, e.g. on the sarcophagus of Adelfia (p. 61, above), the setting of Adam and Eve on their careers of toil by God, and a further stage in the story is shown at the Via Latina, where they sit clad in skins with their sons standing by them, each holding his offering, and the serpent, symbol of the coming murder, is present in the middle of the picture.

39

37 *Domitilla.* In the *arcosolium*, Christ-Orpheus, surrounded by various animals. Above left, the prophet Micah (cf. Micah 5.2, Matt. 2.6); right, Moses striking the rock

38 (*centre, left*) *Peter and Marcellinus.* The Fall

39 (*centre, right*) *Via Latina.* Adam and Eve (to left). Their sons, Abel and Cain bring their offerings to the Lord. The serpent can be seen in the centre (Gen. 4. 3–7)

Leaving these rare examples, we next come to two scenes from the history of the patriarchs that are of great importance, namely, Noah in the ark and Abraham's sacrifice of Isaac. Noah stands in the ark in the attitude of an *orans*; he awaits deliverance, the approach of which is signified by the dove with the olive leaf (though representations in which both dove and raven appear are not unknown). The ark itself is simply an *arca*, a box or chest, which may be on the surface of the sea or may have legs just as a chest in any house might have. It generally has also an opened lid. There is no need to regard what we see as a sort of 'conning tower', below which the hull of the great vessel was in a submarine position! In classical mythology both Danäe and Perseus had been adrift in arks, and Noah may be represented in

an analogous way. But the whole sense is different; the adventures of the individuals Danäe and Perseus do not compare with the world significance of the biblical story. We see a deliverance 'by water' of eight persons, as the First Epistle of Peter (3.10) has it. 'The ambiguous phrase, "by water" is chosen to enable the author to frame an analogy between the waters of the flood and the waters of baptism. We must certainly feel that his language is forced in the extreme when he asks us to think of the water which overwhelmed the earth with destruction as being in any sense the medium of salvation for the inhabitants of the ark.'[28] But the Christians were accustomed to such arbitrary interpretations, as where St Paul (I Cor. 10.12) regards the passage through the Red Sea as a prototype of baptism. The water and the salvation were the important thing. As Cyprian had written in the third century, 'As often as water by itself is mentioned in Holy Scripture, baptism is proclaimed.' Yet the latter scene, i.e. the passage through the Red Sea, is very rare in early Christian art (see p. 70, below).

In the Book of Enoch (44.17–19) and in Philo[29] Noah is regarded as the head of a new humanity. He thus prefigures Christ and is an earnest of the salvation of Christians, who were living surrounded by the waves of persecution. The Flood was a figure of persecution. 'The ark is a type of the Church,' says a third-century writer.[30] The doctrine that there was no salvation outside the Church was at that time a strong dissuasive for heresy and schism.

But the scene that is probably the most common in all forms of early Christian art is the sacrifice of Isaac by his father Abraham

Opposite (bottom)
40 Abraham preparing to sacrifice Isaac (cf. Ill. 41)

41 Jordani. A comprehensive series of pictures which include Jonah under his booth in Nineveh, Daniel, and Abraham sacrificing the ram in place of Isaac

42 *Peter and Marcellinus.* This is a series of contiguous pictures from the Old and the New Testament, showing (left) Moses striking the rock, and the paralytic who has taken up his bed and walks, (right) the healing of the woman with the 'issue of blood', who touched Christ's garments, and Noah in the ark, with both dove and raven. The ark is represented as a chest with legs. Noah stands erect in the attitude of an *orans* (cf. Ill. 29). Above the door was a Christ-Orpheus, now badly damaged

67

43 *Thrason*. This series of contiguous paintings is most comprehensive. They are (upper row) Moses striking the rock, Jesus multiplying the loaves, Epiphany, three *orantes*, Noah, the raising of Lazarus; (lower row) Daniel, Tobias with his fish and the angel, the healing of the paralytic, Job

on Mount Moriah (Gen. 22.1–14). The scene is portrayed with many varieties of detail, some derived from the biblical narrative, others from the artist's imagination, and, besides being common among the paintings of the catacombs, is exceedingly frequent on lamps and sarcophagi. In the passage in Genesis the important point is that God tested Abraham (Gen. 22.1), and the promised blessings were to be granted 'because you have obeyed my voice'. Similarly in the Epistle of James it is the union of faith and works that is the important thing (Jas 2.21–4). But this does not explain why this subject was suitable for funerary art. That explanation is found in the Epistle to the Hebrews (11.17–19), where the faith of Abraham was faith in the Resurrection. 'He considered that God was able to raise men even from the dead: hence figuratively speaking, he did receive him back' (ibid. 19). Once again the scene is one of deliverance, and leads us to the Resurrection and its supreme importance. In one picture a dove appears, the sign of peace and deliverance. This significance surely prevails over a symbolic representation of the Passion.

The incident at Mamre (Gen. 18.1–16), where three celestial visitants came to Abraham, is one to which reference is often made in Christian literature as a manifestation of the working of the Word in the world. This scene became important in Christian (mosaic) art, as the well known examples from Santa Maria Maggiore in Rome, and from San Vitale in Ravenna show. But this scene has little connexion with funerary art, and appears in it once only, at the Via Latina. It may be that attention was drawn to this scene in the minds of Christians by events at Mamre in the reign of Constantine, when, at the prompting of his mother Helena, the Emperor suppressed the immoral rites that flourished at this sacred spot, and built a church to hallow it.

The oppression of the Jewish people in Egypt, their eventual rescue and their adventurous journey to the Promised Land, were the supreme episodes of Jewish history. These happenings involved deliverance from paganism and persecution for the old Israel, wrought, under God, by Moses, and could symbolize, for Christians, the delivery wrought by Christ for the New Israel. This parallel between Christ and Moses had been made from the earliest days of Christianity, and the number of pictures representing Moses at the Via Latina is noteworthy.

In art little attention was paid to Moses' life in Egypt. For his discovery by Pharaoh's daughter we have again to wait for the Via Latina. But the crucial stage in his career, when, at the burning bush on Mount Horeb, he received his commission from God, is represented at least six times in extant catacomb paintings (Ex. 3.4–17). Of these the most notable perhaps is in the catacomb of Callistus. Moses is taking off his shoes. Contiguous to this in St Callistus there is a picture of Moses striking the rock (Ex. 17.6) an incident of which more will be said later. It should perhaps be noted that Moses is bearded in one picture and without beard in the other. God's hand is stretched down to him from heaven, a feature that can be seen (with the hand holding the Law) in one of the two representations of this scene at the Via Latina.

The deliverance of Israel at the Red Sea (Ex. 14) is a scene widely diffused on sarcophagi in different countries, but of which

44

45

44 *Via Latina*. The discovery of the infant Moses by Pharaoh's daughter (Ex. 2. 1–10). 'God' sits to left watching the scene

45 *Via Latina*. The crossing of the Red Sea. In centre, Moses with his wonder-working rod: to left, the Egyptians being overwhelmed: to right, the Hebrews, unarmed, but now assured of safety

there are few examples in paintings. Both Bosio and Aringhi (1650) mention this scene, but the instances to which they refer are now lost. It is once more to the Via Latina that we must turn. Here there are two pictures depicting the deliverance of Israel. We need not be surprised that this event is rarely depicted, because it involves 'crowd' scenes, such as are not a feature of catacomb art. There must be two crowds, of Israelites and of Egyptians, and the latter are in process of being overwhelmed. Before the former Moses stands, holding the rod given him at his commissioning – 'You shall take in your hand this rod, with which you shall do the signs' (Ex. 4.17). He stretched out his hand to render the sea dry (Ex. 14.21), and again to cause the waters to return. The crossing of the sea, as has already been pointed out, was used as an image of baptism by St Paul (I Cor. 10.2, p. 67, above), but whether this image was consciously present in the minds of the painters must be doubtful. It is surely more likely that the scene is one of deliverance from the forces of paganism and persecution.

As the Old Testament narrative shows, Moses (and Aaron) continually suffered from the disbelief of their countrymen, who lapsed into distrust of their leaders on the slightest pretext. In 46 the *Coemeterium Maius* there is a picture that appears to

represent some such incident. The Jews are remonstrating with their leaders. But to what particular incident reference is being made remains uncertain. This picture is unique in catacomb art, but it occurs on sarcophagi. There are other pictures from the wanderings of Israel, illustrative of God's continual protection, but rarely appearing in the catacombs. Moses, receiving the Law out of the cloudy pillar is seen, almost as a space filler, in the upper part of each of two striking pictures of the raising of Lazarus in the Via Latina. This subject is, however, frequently represented on sarcophagi. The gift of manna, one of the most remarkable manifestations of God's mercy, is found but once, in the catacomb of Cyriaca, which is not noted for the number and excellence of its paintings. To the Christian this would represent refreshment on the journey to Paradise, not necessarily the Eucharist, of which there are so many other symbols.

Of all the pictures relating to the wanderings of Israel, by far the most important was Moses striking the rock near Mount Horeb (Ex. 17.2ff.) when the people had no water. This scene became associated in the minds of some Christians with the purifying waters of baptism, more than with water to relieve physical thirst. For the figure(s) which receive the water, when represented, wear Roman military cloaks, and/or the circular

46 *Coemeterium Maius.* Moses and Aaron attacked by their countrymen (as happened quite frequently, cf. Ex. 5, 20–21; 16. 2ff.; 17. 1ff.; 32. 1ff.). But an identification of the occasion is not possible. Moses, with rod, will be the left-hand figure

47

47 *Commodilla*. Moses (Peter) striking the rock. The figures receiving the water are Roman soldiers (see p. 71). The biblical story became conflated with the legend of the miraculous spring which gushed forth in Peter's prison at Rome, and in which he baptized his jailers

48 *Via Latina*. Balaam pointing to the star (Numbers 24. 17). Balaam and the star appear several times in Peter and Marcellinus, and in St Sebastian. As Wilpert points out, the examples in P.M. were supposed, by Bosio and others, to represent Moses receiving the law; cf. also Balaam pointing to the star (Priscilla) in the presence of the Virgin and Child (Ill. 60)

Roman military headgear (*pileus Pannonicus*) which may be seen for instance on the heads of Diocletian and his fellow rulers, on their statues that stand outside St Mark's in Venice. The Old Testament story is thus brought into association with the baptism of Cornelius by or at the command of St Peter (Acts 10.44ff.), or with the myth of the baptism of Peter's jailers in Rome in the fountain that miraculously gushed forth in prison. Moses therefore becomes in some sense identified with Peter. The frequency of this picture must indicate its importance for Christians. Wilpert recorded sixty-eight examples, and others have since been found.

One incident on the journey from Egypt that has left its mark on Christian funerary art is the story of Balaam (Numbers 22ff.).   48
Barak, king of Moab, alarmed at the victorious progress of Israel, sent for Balaam, a renowned 'medicine man', to curse these invaders, 'for I know that he whom you bless is blessed, and he whom you curse is cursed' (ibid. 22.6). Balaam was unwilling to go, but eventually God suffered him to do so, 'but only what I bid you that shall you do' (ibid. 22.20). Twice, at the Via Latina, we find the scene in which the angel, seen by Balaam's ass, but not by its master, blocked the way. This scene appears also, among other reliefs from the Old and New Testaments, on a sarcophagus at St Sebastian. But Balaam was far more important for another reason, for his prophecy of the star (Numbers 24.17, 'A star shall come forth out of Jacob, and a sceptre shall rise out of Israel'). This passage obviously belonged to an early collection of *Testimonia*, passages from the Old Testament relating to the coming of the Messiah, which were used in Christian instruction. Moreover, 'the text is perhaps the most frequently quoted in the Qumran writings. It therefore had a special popularity when the New Testament was being formed.'[31] A figure pointing to a star is portrayed in the catacombs of Peter and Marcellinus and of the Via Latina, but more significant still is the picture in the catacomb of Priscilla of the Virgin and Child,   60
before whom stands a figure pointing to a star. This text from Numbers is found, in the second century, twice in Irenaeus, and twice in Justin; in one of the occasions when Justin uses it, he conflates it with a passage from Isaiah. In the latter prophet the lightening of darkness is also prophesied and visitors from the East, who will bring gold and frankincense (p. 87, below). Thus the story of Baalam not only represents the overriding by God of the powers of evil represented by King Barak (cf. Joshua 24.9–10), but also looks forward to the coming of Christ. Wilpert

49 *Via Latina*. Samson and the lion (Judges, 14. 5ff.). Below, the *dead* lion is shown, with the swarm of bees that gave rise to Samson's riddle (Judges 14. 8ff.)

50 David and his sling: one of the panels in a ceiling in the catacomb of Domitilla. This small-scale picture is the only one of David in surviving catacomb decoration

found another picture of the scene of the Virgin, Child and Prophet in Domitilla, but this one is in a ruined condition.[32]

The history of Israel during the period of the Judges and the Kings has left little trace. Even David appears but little. That his achievements were not forgotten in the third century is shown by the picture of David and Goliath, found at Dura-Europos. In the catacombs we have one picture only of David, seen with his sling, in Domitilla. Wilpert uses this picture to show the economy practised in the use of figures in catacomb paintings. There was plenty of room to include Goliath, if the artist had wished, by excluding two unimportant scenes on either side. But it was enough just to represent David, with his sling.

The ascent of Elijah to heaven, by which he escaped the common fate of death, is a subject we might expect to find. But it has been found twice only, once in Domitilla, and once at the Via Latina. In both pictures the chariot with Elijah, which has just taken off, is seen towards the centre; Elisha, receiving his master's mantle, is on the left; to the right is a spectator, perhaps included for the sake of symmetry, but prominent enough to have a real significance which now escapes us. It is easy to make a comparison of the chariot of Elijah with that of the Sun God, and Wilpert made an additional comparison to the coins struck at the death of Constantine, on which the Emperor ascends to heaven

in a chariot, and a hand is stretched out from heaven to receive him. It may also be recalled that on a mosaic in a tomb of the cemetery under St Peter's, Christ/Helios is represented in his chariot. Again, in a picture in Peter and Marcellinus, between two scenes illustrating the story of Jonah, Christ/Helios appears.

The narration of the Book of Jonah is a subject very frequently represented. It is usually depicted in three or four scenes: (1) Jonah being precipitated from the ship into the waiting mouth of the 'whale', a sea monster whose anatomy would receive a human body only with difficulty; (2) the (vigorous) ejection of Jonah ('it vomited out Jonah, 3.10); (3 and/or 4) Jonah under his 'booth', or the plant which God had sent to shade him, and Jonah angry with his commission from God (4.1) or with the plant (4.8–9), which had withered.

The series of pictures are so placed that they may be taken in almost at a glance: they are frequently located in panels of the ceiling in *cubicula*, accompanied by other such pictures, e.g. of Noah or Daniel. The most obvious significance of the story, in a funerary context, is that given by our Lord in Matthew, 12.39ff., where the experience of Jonah is enunciated as a figure of the resurrection. (The difficulties about the accuracy of this prefiguring, particularly in view of the Lucan parallel (11.29–30) do not really concern us here.) We can thus, however, account

51 *Via Latina*. The ascension of Elijah (2 Kings 2. 9ff.). To left is Elisha receiving the mantle of Elijah, to right, a spectator; his presence may be simply to give symmetry to the scene, of the representation in Domitilla (Wilpert, Pl. 230. 2). But he may have a significance that now escapes us

75

52 *Peter and Marcellinus.* Ceiling of a *cubiculum.* In centre, Daniel; at top, Noah: left, right and bottom, the story of Jonah. In corners, deer in landscape. The story of Jonah is here represented in three scenes, the throwing of Jonah from the ship is omitted

for two only of the pictures. The third and fourth are set in Nineveh whither the Lord has sent Jonah to preach 'Repent or else ...' The purport of pictures three and four is simply to complete the story told in this short book. It has been suggested that the picture of Jonah reclining under his 'booth' is taken from pagan representations of Endymion. But such a resemblance may mean no more than that a reclining male figure resembles any other reclining male figure.

53   Job appears about a dozen times in catacomb paintings. He usually is a solitary seated figure, but sometimes his wife is also shown, offering him food on a rod or stick, and not touching him because of the loathsome sores that afflict him. Job had been noted as a symbol of resurrection early in Christian history, in I Clement (*c.* AD 96), referring to Job 19.26, albeit in an errant version, and he also served as an example of suffering who was eventually vindicated, and could thus be regarded as a type of Christ himself. Origen also mentions Job as an example of steadfastness. 'If I have laid my hand on my mouth to kiss,' i.e. to show respect to a heathen god, 'let this also be reckoned to me as the greatest crime' (Job 31.27, quoted in *Exhortation to Martyrdom,* 33).

53 *Domitilla.* Job

54

54 Marcus and Marcellianus. The three young men refuse to worship the idol at the order of King Nebuchadrezzar. Above is the signature of Bosio, who left similar record of his explorations at other places also (see Ill. 71)

Christians were clearly impressed by scenes from the period of the Jewish exile in Mesopotamia. From the fact that Hippolytus early in the third century produced a commentary on the Book of Daniel we can see that this book must have held an interest for Roman Christians. Four scenes are involved: the refusal of the young men to obey the king's command to worship the image that he had set up (Daniel, 3) and their subsequent committal to the furnace; Daniel in the lion's den, and the story of Susanna. All these are peculiarly apposite to the very situation of Christians in the centuries of persecution, who could suffer death by being burnt alive, or by the beasts in the arena, or who in the case of girls could be subjected to sexual outrage. References to the deliverance of the young men, of Daniel and of Susanna, occur so frequently in funeral liturgies that, even though the latter are of later date than our pictures, one may judge that such examples were used at a much earlier date in the burial of the dead.

54-57

54

The refusal of Shadrach, Meshach and Abednego, i.e. Ananias, Azarias and Misael, to worship the image set up by

55 *Priscilla*. The three young men in the furnace (Daniel 3. 8ff.). Note the eastern hats, cf. Daniel (ibid. 21) where hats are mentioned, and the dove, the sign of deliverance, flying over them. They stand in the posture of *orantes*

56 *Priscilla (Cappella Greca)*. The story of Susanna. On right, the elders lay their hands on Susanna's head (Susanna, 34): on left, Daniel comes to aid Susanna. Both stand in the posture of *orantes*

Nebuchadrezzar (Daniel, 3) is both shown in pictures and frequent on Christian lamps and sarcophagi. The image is suspiciously like the bust of a Roman emperor and the king wears Roman uniform; the image is certainly not, as the Book of Daniel says, 'sixty cubits high and six cubits broad'. The three young men, cast into the furnace, stand in the attitude of *orantes*; they seldom have the companionship of the fourth figure, whom the king saw in the fire 'like a son of the gods' (Daniel 3.25). But the figure appears once, in Domitilla; in Priscilla a dove flies over the young men, and in the *Coemeterium Maius* a hand is stretched down to them from above. Origen writing his *Exhortation to Martyrdom* about AD 235 mentions the ordeal of the young men as apposite to Christians of his day, who are the true hebrews and are still threatened by Nebuchadrezzar, now represented by Emperor Maximinus (235–8), who caused among others Origen's friend Ambrose to suffer. In the middle of the fourth century, when catacomb art was perhaps at its most flourishing, Liberius, Bishop of Rome cited the three young men as an example of the resistance that he was himself then offering to Constantius II.[33]

57 *Praetextatus*. The *arcosolium* of Celerina, whose name is preserved in an inscription which ran along the top. In the foreground Susanna, figured as a lamb, is being persecuted by the elders (SENIORIS) figured as wolves. To right and left, figures of saints. The letters LIB beside the head of the figure on the right probably identify him as Liberius, Bishop of Rome 352–66

Daniel stands, usually naked, in the attitude of an *orans* with a lion on either side; the lions vary, sometimes they snarl, sometimes they look exceedingly docile ('God sent His angel and shut the lions' mouths,' Dan. 6.22). Obviously there were in reality more than two lions – in the second account of Daniel's adventure given in the *Story of Bel and the Dragon* 'there were seven lions in the den' – but the symmetrical approach, with as few figures as possible, is typical of catacomb painting. The den, in the Latin text of Daniel, was obviously a hollow, a LACUS LEONUM, but occasionally Daniel is shown standing on a ridge, just as martyrs would in the arena. Garruchi[34] thought that Daniel represented Christ, and the ridge Calvary. One must not, however, insist upon this. Wilpert regarded it as nothing more than a means of assisting the artist to fill symmetrically the space available to him.

The story of Susanna, wife of Joachim, is found in one of the additions to the Book of Daniel now included in the Apocrypha. The points on which the Christians fastened were the accusation of Susanna by the two wicked elders, and her vindication by Daniel. Pictures are found at Rome in six catacombs. Hippolytus, in the commentary mentioned above, adopted a figurative explanation: 'Susanna prefigured the Church and Joachim her husband, Christ, and the garden the calling of the saints, who are planted like fruitful trees in the Church. And Babylon is the world, and the two elders are set forth as a figure of the two peoples that plot against the Church, i.e. Jews and Gentiles.'

Susanna, with an elder on either side, stands in the garden in the attitude of an *orans* (Peter and Marcellinus, and the *Coemeterium Maius*). In Priscilla there are two scenes, in one the elders have placed their hands on Susanna's head (Susanna 34) not, as Hippolytus says 'that at least by touching her they might satisfy their lust', but in 'the symbolic act of witnesses before the stoning'.[35] Contiguous to this is a picture of Daniel with Susanna, whom he has come to rescue, a thing which he accomplished by convicting the elders of discrepant testimony. (See also p. 84, below.)

In Praetextatus the scene is figurative: Susanna is a lamb, and the *seniores* are wolves; the identification is certain, as they are named in the picture. There is also a picture in the catacomb of Thecla, which may refer to the story. A man is dragging off a woman, 'as she was being led away to be put to death ...' (Susanna 45). But this identification is problematical. It is clear, however, that the Roman Christians were familiar with, and valued, the story of Susanna's deliverance.

An incident in the story of Tobias and the angel, as recorded in the Book of Tobit, was illustrated three times in the catacomb of Thrason, once in Domitilla (seen by Bosio and others, but now destroyed) and once at the Via Latina. This book was, from the second century onwards, in common use among Christians as well as among the Jews: 'it must have held in Jewish households much the position once held by Bunyan's *Pilgrim's Progress* in our own.'[36] Its date is probably about the second century BC. But from the whole story of this 'romance' we are concerned only with Tobias and the monster fish from the river Tigris which nearly swallowed him, but which was caught by him at the behest of his friend the angel: from its internal organs came magic powers that served Tobias well (Tobit 6.1ff.). Now, the fish represented in one of the pictures in the catacomb of Thrason is no monster. It is a very ordinary fish that few anglers would boast of catching. Here it may be that the variant reading found in the text of the Aramaic and of one Hebrew version, 'and devoured the young man's bread', represents the version known to those who introduced this picture to the catacomb. It was 'an attempt to lessen the improbability of the story'.[37] The fish once depicted in Domitilla was also quite small:[38] in the other pictures from Thrason and in the Via Latina it is of more respectable dimensions, but no man-eater. Naturally the fish eventually led on to thoughts of Christ, the divine fish. But this first appears in Optatus (3.2) towards the end of the fourth century. The story of Tobias therefore is again one of deliverance on a journey wrought with the help of an angel.

We finally turn to the 'new' catacomb on the Via Latina, where the number and variety of the pictures from the Old Testament take us far beyond the usual subjects of catacomb decoration. The usual, we may say the conventional, pictures are there, and a few of the new pictures have been already mentioned, where occasion demanded. Now we shall briefly look at the other scenes. The stories of the patriarchs in Genesis, and the story of Moses had a particular interest. There are pictures of the drunkenness of Noah (Gen. 9.20–21), the flight of Lot from Sodom (19.15–26), the meal of Isaac and his blessing of Jacob 58 (27.1–22) (twice), Jacob's vision at Bethel (28.10–13), the dreams of Joseph (37.5–10), Joseph's meeting with his brethren 59 (42.6–8), the arrival of Jacob and his household in Egypt (46.5–27), Jacob's blessing of Ephraim and Manasseh (48). Pictures illustrating the career of Moses have already been mentioned, but the further history of Israel is enlarged by the episode of Phineas, grandson of Aaron (Numbers 25.6–15), who (dressed as a Roman) is transfixing Zimri and Cozbi with a spear, a deed by which the house of Aaron gained God's promise of an everlasting priesthood. The story of Samson attracted attention in the episodes of his killing the lion (Judges 14.5–9), his setting fire to the fields of the Philistines (15.4–5) and his slaying of the Philistines with the jaw-bone of an ass (15.14–16). An isolated scene from the story of David shows Absalom hanging from the oak tree (II Kings 18.9).

Now, while these pictures are new in catacomb art, some of them at any rate were appearing in other art forms of contemporary, or not much later dates.[39] Among them are ones that have no funerary significance whatever. Some of them appear in a literary source like the *Dittochaeon* of Prudentius (late fourth century), where a collection of four-line stanzas describes scenes from both Testaments which probably appeared in paintings or mosaics in a church. It is hazardous to postulate any definite source for these paintings and their uniqueness is emphasized by the fact that, in other catacombs which were in use in the fourth century, no such pictures are found. This catacomb was not public[40] but belonged to a restricted circle of wealthy families, who may reflect the interest of the society in which the biblical studies of Jerome flourished around AD 365.

In an article[41] Josef Fink has emphasized the influence of the Old Testament on the pictures of this catacomb. A much

58 *Via Latina*. Jacob at
Bethel: his vision of the
heavenly ladder and the
angels ascending and
descending (Gen. 28)

59 *Via Latina*. Jacob
blessing Ephraim and
Manasseh, the sons of
Joseph (Gen. 48)

damaged picture, thought by Ferrua to be an Annunciation, has been identified by Fasola (cf. Fink, p. 6) as the episode of Judah and Tamar in Genesis 38.12–18; the Sermon on the Mount (cf. Ill. 77) is the giving of the Law by Moses;[42] a picture of Christ and the Apostles is a second scene of the story of Susanna, i.e. there are two pictures, just as there are in the representation of the same story in Priscilla (see p. 81, above); in the second scene Daniel is preparing to rescue Susanna (Daniel 13.46ff., Susanna 45). The picture mentioned already as portraying the coming of the flood is interpreted as Rahab and the spies (Joshua 2). The striking picture of Jesus and the woman of Samaria at the well is interpreted as the meeting of the outcast Hagar and the angel in the desert (Gen. 16.6ff.) on the ground that the male figure is not in any sense weary, as Jesus was in the Gospel narrative; and the anatomy lesson (pp. 128–9, below) is the death of King Asa of Judah (cf. I Kings 15.23–4, 2 Chron. 16.7). 'Asa' has no feet depicted ('But in his old age he was diseased in his feet' (I Kings 15.23)), whereas the other figures have! No opinion is here expressed with regard to these identifications, but they certainly are interesting.

6

The New Testament and the Catacombs

I tell you that, if these should hold their peace, the stones would immediately cry out.

Luke 19.40. A.V.

We have now seen the extent to which scenes from the Old Testament contributed to the decoration of the catacombs; the influence and importance to Christianity of its Jewish background are clear, but we must now consider what elements in Christianity itself were portrayed on Christian tombs. Naturally the material comes in great measure from the New Testament, but to begin with we can take a look at one link between the old and the new. That link is the star, prophesied by Balaam, and now actualized by the star which led the Magi on their journey in search of the infant king (Matt. 2.1–12). We have already mentioned the scene in the catacomb of Priscilla where the prophet stands before the seated Virgin and her Child and points to the star, a scene which also occurs in a much mutilated picture 60
in Domitilla.[43] The Annunciation itself is portrayed, however, in the catacomb of Priscilla. The angel, unwinged as angels are in 61
the art of this period, stands before the Virgin with his right hand raised, as a sign that he is speaking, or a sign of power. The identification of this scene was one that the early investigators of the catacombs were slow to reach. Bosio discovered the picture, but both he and Aringhi were doubtful as to its meaning, and it was Bottari who first suggested that it might be an Annunciation; Garruchi positively identified it, and Wilpert found a similar picture in Peter and Marcellinus. Here therefore we begin with the narrative of St Luke's Gospel, but there is no follow-up. The adoration of the shepherds at the manger, where the animals in the stable appear, is very rarely represented. It was the subject of one picture, now practically destroyed, at St Sebastian and of a fresco, now mutilated, in Peter and Marcellinus; it also occurs on the sarcophagus of Adelfia.

60 *Priscilla*. The prophet
Balaam before the Virgin
and Child. He is pointing
to the star (Numbers 24.
17)

61 *Priscilla*. The
Annunciation. This is the
earliest example of what
became a most important
feature of Christian Art.
The Virgin is, as usual,
seated

62 *Coemeterium Maius.*
The Virgin and Child.
The Virgin is in the
attitude of an *orans*

But the scene from the stories of the birth of Jesus that is
universal is the visit of the Magi. This scene cannot have a
funereal meaning, nor is it, directly, a theme of deliverance. In a
picture in Peter and Marcellinus the Magi are seen alone,
greeting the star, which is in the shape of a primitive Chi-rho
monogram. 'When they saw the star, they rejoiced with
exceeding great joy.' (Matt. 2.10). In Cyriaca also a figure points
to the star, and its importance is further emphasized in a picture
from the catacomb of Marcus and Marcellianus in which the
seated Christ appears with four standing figures, one of whom,
presumably the evangelist Matthew, points to a star.[44]

In the generally depicted scene, in which three Magi present
their gifts to the seated Virgin and Child, what is portrayed is the
recognition of the Divine Infant, but by whom? The Eastern
provenance of the Magi is recognized in their Eastern garb. They   30
wear the well-known 'Phrygian' caps, and their garments are
sometimes resplendent with colour. Their coming could be
regarded as the earliest recognition of Christ by Gentiles, or
simply as a fulfilment of Old Testament prophecy (Isaiah 60.3,
6) or as the subservience of the powers of magic, as Ignatius
wrote, to the power of Christ (Ephesians 19). 'The idea that
magic was overthrown by the Advent of Christ is frequent in the
Fathers, and this overthrow was commonly connected, as here,
with the visit and worship of the Magi, as the symbol and
assurance of its defeat.'[45] In the Matthean story the gifts (Matt.
2.11) foreshadow the divinity, the royalty and the death of
Christ. Hence the three gifts require three Magi to present them.
But the number three was not essential, and considerations of
symmetry, or simply lack of space, could bring the number down
to two, or, for the first of these reasons, increase it to four.

There are two other scenes on which the Child is depicted.
On an *arcosolium* in the *Coemeterium Maius*, the Virgin is   62

87

63 *Priscilla*. In centre, an *orans*. To right, the Virgin with the Divine Child; to left, a virgin receiving the veil. (Both the *orans* and the virgin receiving the veil presumably represent the person buried in this *arcosolium*.) At bottom, signature of Bosio

64 *Callistus*. The baptism of Jesus; to left, a fisherman; to right, the paralytic carrying his bed, an event often associated with baptism (from the account in John 5. 2–9)

represented as an *orans*. She is magnificently dressed, with necklace, earrings and veil. The Child sits on her lap, but has now passed well beyond babyhood. The Child is not in the attitude of an *orans*. On either side is the Chi-rho monogram, the presence of which, with the adornment vouchsafed to Mary, dates the picture to the fourth century. The import of the picture is that Mary is adding her prayers to those of the relatives of the dead.

The other scene is found in the catacomb of Priscilla where, according to the usual interpretation, a consecrated virgin is receiving the veil, in the presence of the Virgin, who holds the Child, this time a naked infant. She is, as St Ambrose said, the pattern of the virgin's state and an example for all. (*De Virg.* 2.2). But this interpretation of the picture, in a funereal setting, is not without its difficulties.

The baptism of Jesus is depicted four times in extant catacomb painting. This event marked the beginning of his ministry, just as, for the individual Christian, baptism marked the beginning of his new life in Christ. As we have seen, baptism is symbolized in pictures other than those of the actual event, in particular those of the Flood and of Moses striking the rock. Tertullian in his work *On baptism* mentions the latter, the healing of the paralytic at the pool of Bethesda (Jn 5.2–9), and Elisha's purification of water (II Kings 2.18–22) as types of baptism.

Pictures of the baptism of Jesus are easily distinguishable by the descent of the dove. Probably the earliest of these pictures comes from the crypt of Lucina. Jesus is a young adult, and the Baptist is helping him from the Jordan at the moment after baptism. In the other pictures of Jesus' baptism he is smaller in stature than the Baptist, and in two pictures the latter is pouring the water over him from his hand, a method not unknown in the early Church. Moreover the only picture in which Jesus is in the posture of an *orans* is in a scene of baptism from Peter and Marcellinus. That is in accordance with the narrative of Luke (3.21). 'Jesus also having been baptized and praying . . .'

It should also be noted that in art baptism is brought into close connexion with the Eucharist. As an example of this we have the picture of the wedding at Cana (Jn 2.1–11), in an *arcosolium* in Peter and Marcellinus, where beside it there is a picture of baptism, though not necessarily of Jesus. (See also top of page.) This connexion is natural, because a newly baptized person would, as we see from Justin and Hippolytus, receive the Eucharist for the first time immediately; baptism and Eucharist

65 *Peter and Marcellinus.* The wedding at Cana. Jesus is touching the jars with his wonder-working staff. To left, a scene of baptism; above, an *orans*; to right, Moses striking the rock, a scene also symbolic of baptism

64

65

were really parts of *one* ceremony of initiation. Hence the descriptions of the first eucharist that the above-named authors give, separating it from the normal Sunday celebration. The latter was constantly to be repeated, the former was once for all.

There is nothing funereal in the baptism of Jesus, whereas there is in the baptism of the Christian, because it marked his death to sin and his rising to life eternal. Wilpert began his account of baptism in the catacomb paintings by referring to the inscription of Antonia Cyriaca at the entrance to the basilica of Marcus and Marcellianus. This girl died at the age of nineteen 'on the fourth day after she received the grace of God', i.e. after baptism. This was the 'seal' which marked out the faith which led to the Resurrection, or as Aphraates, the Persian sage, put it, 'The Holy Ghost, through baptism enters a man, and gives him resurrection.'[46]

Linked to the scene of baptism is the fisherman. The disciples were to be 'fishers of men' (Matt. 4.9, Mark 1.17), and a fisherman appears several times in catacomb paintings. Christ is called 'fisher of men that are being saved', in the well-known hymn of Clement of Alexandria. But ideas crowd in one upon another. 'We', said Tertullian 'are the little tiddlers', in contrast to the great fish Christ (i.e. *ichthys*, Jesus Christos Theou Uios Soter). 'We are born in the water, nor otherwise are we safe than by remaining in it.' The idea of Christ as the fish prevailed over that of the fisherman.

Fish also was included, and that almost universally, in representations of a sacred meal, whether it be the Eucharist, a funeral feast, or the banquet of the blessed in heaven. This is the case also in the inscription of Avircius Marcellus, who, on his travels from Asia Minor to Rome, 'received, with bread and wine, the fish from the spring – immense, pure, which the pure Virgin caught and gave to her friends to eat for ever . . .'

The inclusion of the fish at the sacred meal was appropriate in view of the fact that, as we have just seen, Christ was regarded as the fish, and fish had been provided at the feeding of the 5,000, and by the risen Lord at the lakeside (Jn 21). Particularly fine examples are the pictures of fish and bread in the Crypt of Lucina. Unfortunately the central part of this picture, between the two fish, has been destroyed; it may have represented the Eucharist. The sacred meal will receive further consideration later on. In the meanwhile we shall consider first the miracles of Christ, and then his teaching as it is revealed in the catacomb paintings.

66

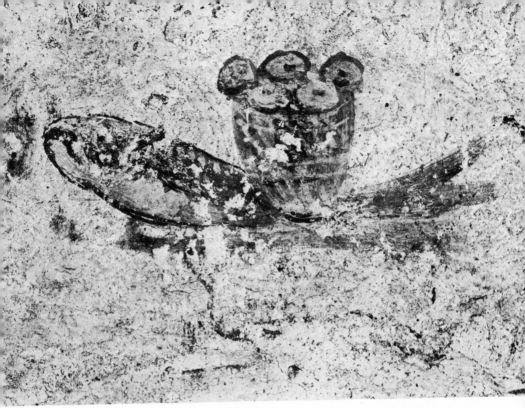

The miracles may be divided into two classes, those which are straightforward miracles of deliverance, and those which have a wider import. The former class, apart from the healing of the paralytic, to which reference has already been made (Matt. 9.2–8, Mk 2.3–12, Luke 5.18–26, Jn 5.2–9), do not amount to much. The others represented are the healings (1) of the woman with an issue of blood (Matt. 9.20–22, Mk 5.25–34, Luke 8. 43–8), (2) of the blind man (Mk 8.22–6 and 10.46–52, Jn 9.1–7), (3) of the leper (Matt. 8.2–4, Mk 1.40–44, Luke 5.12–14), (4) of the Gadarene demoniac. There are four examples of the first-named, one in Praetextatus, and three in Peter and Marcellinus. The example in Praetextatus is nearer to the account in the Gospels. The scene was obviously a 'crowd' scene, and two other persons are shown with Jesus. In the other three examples Jesus and the woman are singled out and are alone, a circumstance that coincides with the usual principle of catacomb painting.

Seven copies exist, or are known to have existed, of the healing of the blind man; but we cannot be certain as to whether any specific healing is meant. Christ is represented as laying his hand on the head of the man, as in Mk 8.22–5.

It is hardly worth going into the representation of the healing of the leper, and of the healing of the Gadarene demoniac. Only

66 *Callistus*. The Eucharist: bread and fish; a receptacle on the side of the basket may contain wine. This is in fact one of a pair of similar pictures

67 *Via Latina*. The raising of Lazarus. The artist has overcome the difficulty of representing a crowd. Above, the cloud and the pillar, and Moses about to receive the law

68 The raising of Lazarus, from a 'gold-glass' vessel. Lazarus is still bound by the grave clothes

one copy survives of the former, and the identification of the latter scene in two supposed pictures given by Wilpert is uncertain. The older investigators (Bosio, Aringhi and Bottari) thought that one of these pictures represented Christ's blessing of the children (Matt. 19.13ff., Mk 10.13ff., Luke 18.15ff.).

The healing miracles, therefore, yield very little but it is important to note that where they occur they are mostly concerned with faith in Jesus as the Son of God, as the divine deliverer. The 'nature' miracles, e.g. the stilling of the storm, appear not at all. Such miracles were however not unknown to art as the representation at Dura of Jesus and Peter walking on the water shows.

But of all the miracles of Jesus, the raising of Lazarus (Jn 11) is that which has by far the greatest impact on the art of the catacombs. Wilpert mentioned 53 examples, and others have been discovered since he wrote. This miracle was the most striking example of Jesus' power over death. As such, we cannot wonder at its frequency, but we may comment on how seldom other similar miracles, like the raising of Jairus' daughter (Matt. 9.18–26, Mk 5.21–24, 35–43, Luke 8.41–2, 49–56), and of the son of the widow of Nain, (Luke 7.11–16) appear on paintings.

In the representation of the raising of Lazarus, there are

69 *Peter and Marcellinus.*
The multiplication of the
loaves

variations of detail. The tomb is not a cave, as the Gospel says (Jn 11.38), but a free-standing building, a tomb such as could be seen standing beside the main roads leading out of Rome, or in any cemetery above ground. It is generally approached by steps, or by a ramp. The only figure that needs to be depicted is Jesus, holding his wonder-working staff and with his right hand raised; but Lazarus may appear emerging from, or outside the tomb, i.e. the scene is portrayed just before or after the utterance of the momentous words, 'Lazarus, come forth' (Jn 11.43). Lazarus is sometimes still bound hand and foot with grave clothes, sometimes Jesus has given the command, 'Loose him, and let him go' (Jn 11.44).

The scene as here described is in accord with the principles of catacomb painting, i.e. to reduce the figures to a minimum; but in the gospel a crowd is present and this feature is represented in the two magnificent representations of this miracle at the Via Latina. As in other pictures in this catacomb, the artists here had no difficulty in representing crowds, and mark a departure from 67 the usual economy of figures. The raising of Lazarus, then, prefigured the victory of Christ over death. Christ was the Life. He is the Way in another oft-represented miracle, the multiplication of the loaves. The provision of the loaves, while 69 drawing its origin from the narrative of the feeding of the 5,000, was not meant as provision for any normal meal.

As Wilpert pointed out long ago, scenes representing banquets are of three kinds: (1) a Eucharist or an Agape, (2) a funeral banquet, (3) the banquet of the blessed ones in heaven. The material available to the artists was limited in such a way that these varying types of banquet are not kept separate. The material for one crowds in on the material for the others.

Wilpert gives 38 examples of the multiplication of the loaves. The act of Jesus is once more isolated, i.e. not done in the presence of the 5,000, who were soon to be partakers of the true bread of heaven (Jn 6.32); it is otherwise with the (much less frequent) representation of the wedding at Cana, where the guests are present, and Jesus is touching wine jars, not baskets, with his wonder-working staff.

'How can this man give us his flesh to eat?' was the question of the Jews, mostly temporary adherents of Christ (Jn 6.52), and his reply was quite unequivocal. 'He that eateth my flesh and drinketh my blood hath eternal life, and I will raise him up at the last day' (Jn 6.54). The actual feeding of the 5,000 was not simply an act of compassion and power, but an event in which the immediate satisfaction of bodily needs is a symbol of something greater. 'Unless ye eat the flesh of the Son of Man and drink his blood, you have no life in you' (Jn 6.53). This teaching reached its consummation in the Last Supper, where Jesus identified the bread and wine with his body and blood, finally enunciating teaching that he may often have given on other occasions. The command to continue the remembrance of his death was one which the disciples took up at once (Acts 2.42), and the aberrations that could follow were pointedly censured by St Paul (I Cor. 11.17ff.).

The most striking example of a eucharistic picture is the so-called 'fractio panis' from the catacomb of Priscilla. The figure seated (as one looks at the picture) at the extreme left, is in the act of breaking the bread. This scene represents in a way that other pictures do not, the moment at which the bishop or presbyter reached the most solemn moment of the service. Similarly in St Callistus we see a consecration scene where a man (? Christ), in presence of an *orans*, lays his hand on bread and fish placed upon a small table.

No area of the catacombs speaks more eloquently of the Eucharist than the 'chapels of the sacraments' in St Callistus where the rite is repeatedly represented with other suitable

70 *Priscilla* (*Cappella Greca*). The Eucharist. *Fractio panis*: to left and right, baskets of bread. In front of the table, a cup and plates with fish and bread

71 *Peter and Marcellinus.* The heavenly banquet. The participants call to the servants, Irene (Peace) and Agape (Love): DA CALDA ('give it warm') or MISCE MI ('mix it for me'!). Above are the 'signatures' of Bosio and Pomponius Letus (see pp. 47, 51)

pictures in close proximity. Most striking of all perhaps are the two pictures already mentioned, of fish, bread and wine in the area known as the crypt of Lucina, originally a separate burial place.

But not only did Christ ordain a sacred meal for his followers in this world, but he also promised them that he and they should eat and drink together in the kingdom of God. 'I tell you, I shall not again drink of this fruit of the vine until that day when I drink it new with you in my Father's kingdom' (Matt. 26.29), or 'they shall come from the east and west, and from the north and south and shall sit down in the kingdom of God' (Luke 13.29, cf. Matt. 8.11). This idea was not unfamiliar to his hearers, as the remark made by one of 'them that sat at meat with him' shows, namely 'Blessed is he that shall eat bread in the kingdom of God' (Luke 14.15); there follows the parable of the great supper (Luke 14.16–24). Now, there are numerous banquet scenes particularly in Peter and Marcellinus, that reproduce such teaching, joyous scenes where the participants call on the servants, who carry names like Agape and Irene, to mix the wine for them or 'give it warm'. This anticipation was not confined to catholic Christians. One of the most notable examples is in the syncretistic catacomb of Vibia, to which reference will be made below (pp. 120–2).

The custom of having funeral feasts at the graves of the dead on their anniversaries was common in the ancient world, and was taken up by the Christians. For them an even stronger motive of commemoration was at hand in the remembrance of the martyrs. In connexion with this we can call to mind the celebration of St Peter and St Paul at the site *ad Catacumbas* on the Via Appia Antica (pp. 31–3, above). At the *Cappella Greca* too, a stone bench

71

72 Coemeterium Maius. One of the thrones for festivals of the dead. Note the architectural detail above

can be seen which must have been used on such occasions. Even more striking are the thrones found in the *Coemeterium Maius*. 72 But these were probably not meant for the living but for the dead, who were the unseen participators at their own commemoration. An inscription of the year 375 states that Florentinus, Fortunatus and Felix came to drink (*ad calicem*) in the catacomb of Priscilla. Finally, a feature of Maltese catacombs, even of very small ones, is the circular '*agape* table' at 123 which the family and friends could recline to partake of their meal. All such celebrations must have enhanced the solidarity of the family with their dead, and in a wider context, the festivals of the Apostles and martyrs must have emphasized the unity of the Christian fellowship.

Quite clearly the artists and/or those who commissioned representations of feasts, whether for paintings or reliefs on sarcophagi, felt a great impulse or need to reproduce such scenes. They were limited by their skill and their space. The participants do not number more than seven. Occasionally the table and the guests are repeated in close proximity again and again, as at St Sebastian (see Ill. 94). This may be an attempt to show something in which a great number participated. They recline or sit at S-shaped tables (*stibadium*) before which are set out bread, fish, and sometimes a cup; these are what Avircius Marcellus habitually received on his travels, *c.* AD 180.

Funeral feasts were not occasions of sadness. As we know from literary evidence, such celebrations, called in Africa *laetitiae*, could turn into riotous orgies which called down on them the wrath of Tertullian at any rate in his Montanist period, and later the criticism of St Ambrose and St Augustine, 'rioting and drunkenness (Rom. 3.13) . . . are practised not only on holy days, when the blessed martyrs are honoured – lamentable sight . . .' (Ep. 22.3). But the whole attitude of Christians to death in the early centuries was not coloured by apprehension. 'The attitude of Christian people towards the departed underwent a subtle but far-reaching change somewhere round the year 1000 . . . The change was, broadly, one from glad confidence in the love of God to an emphasis on God the just and terrible judge . . . "How often", says Cyprian (*De Mortalitate*, 20) "has it been revealed to us . . . that our brothers who have been released from the world by the Divine summons ought not to be mourned for, since we know that they are not lost but gone before; while appearing to lose they have really gained ground, as travellers and navigators are wont to do." '[47]

73 *Priscilla*. The Good
Shepherd

But of all pictures found in catacombs by far the most frequent
and the most striking are representations of the 'good shepherd'.
These pictures are universal. The idea of God as shepherd of his
people is deeply inwrought into the Old Testament in psalm and
prophecy (e.g. Ps. 23, 78, 80, 100, and in Isaiah, Jeremiah and
Ezekiel). The image of Christ as shepherd was taken up in St
John's Gospel, and to this is allied the reference to the lost sheep
and its master in St Matthew and St Luke. Moreover the idea of
Christ as shepherd appears in Acts, I Peter and Hebrews, in the
Martyrium Polycarpi (19.2) and in the oft-mentioned inscription
of Avircius; and *The Shepherd* was the name of the prophetical
work of Hermas, produced at Rome in the first half of the second
century.

In catacomb art the shepherd is generally placed in a 'country'
setting with trees and plants. The shepherd is portrayed in three
73 different roles: (1) He carries the sheep on his shoulders, the lost
sheep of Matthew and Luke (Matt. 18.12–13; Luke 15.5); (2) he
pastures his flock as in Psalm 23 and in John 10, or guards them
74 as in the latter passage; (3) he milks his sheep as any shepherd
might. And while we are on the subject of sheep, we may

74 *Praetextatus*. The shepherd defends his flock from a wild ass and a wild boar

mention, in passing, the idea of Christ himself as the Lamb of God. That belongs to a different cycle of ideas, but one which is also a vital element in the Christian religion.

Representations of a man carrying a sheep go back as far as 1000 BC, to Carchemish and the Hittites. But these sheep are offerings and the forerunners of the *Criophorus* statues of Classical art. The Christian shepherd however does not intend to sacrifice, but to save the sheep, to bring it back to the safety of the fold. We have already mentioned (p. 56) 'shepherds' on 'gold-glass' cups, which as Tertullian pointed out, and as would be obvious even without his testimony, are not the same as the Christian shepherd. Similarly, such figures are found on sarcophagi that are not Christian. These are construed to represent *humanitas* or *philanthropia*. In this sense they have a link with the Christian Good Shepherd, whose function is to save. But they do not explain the latter. The biblical references are a far surer background. The action of the shepherd may be linked to the Christian either in this world or in the next. In this world the Christian is brought back from sinning and is forgiven, in the next his soul is carried to heaven.

74 *Praetextatus*. The shepherd defends his flock from a wild ass and a wild boar

If we may now turn aside for a moment to matters of history, about the year 200 the forgiveness of sins was a question of crucial importance to the Roman Christians, with Callistus on the side of leniency, and Hippolytus on the side of rigorism. When Matthew Arnold wrote of the Church

> On those walls subterranean where she hid
> Her head mid ignominy, death and tombs
> She her good shepherd's hasty image drew
> And on his shoulders not a lamb, a kid,[48]

he was referring to something that is an echo of a picture in the catacomb of Priscilla where the shepherd carried an animal that is no kid, but a large goat, while beside him is a sheep on his right hand, a goat on his left. The he-goat was an animal noted for its lust; the sins about which Callistus and Hippolytus disputed were mostly sexual. Having got thus far it is as well to admit that we are now on problematical matters, which can be regarded, by whoever wishes, as bordering on fantasy.

73

In Praetextatus the shepherd is defending his flock against a wild ass and a wild boar, the 'personifications' of the devil and of moral impurity. This picture is unique but accords completely with the devotion of the shepherd to his flock, as portrayed in St John – 'he lays down his life for the sheep' (10.11).

74

When the shepherd is represented with his flock they are usually in 'green pastures' of luxuriant vegetation. The shepherd may be carrying a sheep, or he may sit beside his flock. The scene is reminiscent of the words in St John's Gospel on the abundant life of the flock (10.10), of the sheep 'going in and out and finding pasture' (10.9).

> Where leaves of green herbs brightly glance
> And in the grove the palm-trees dream,
> And laurels shade the eddying dance
> Of crystal stream,

as Prudentius wrote in his description of a scene such as is now described.[49]

A more classical element is not however wanting, for the shepherd often carries a shepherd's pipe, just as he would in the *Idylls* of Theocritus or the *Eclogues* of Vergil. The Word of God, personified in the shepherd, is a maker of music, as Clement of Alexandria pointed out in his *Protrepticus*: 'but different is my minstrel, for He has come to bring to a speedy end the bitter slavery of the demons that lord it over us.'

From this it is but a step to the portrayal of Christ as Orpheus, who charmed by his music the whole variety of wild nature. Twice, to be sure, the connection of the shepherd with Orpheus is clearly shown in St Callistus and in Peter and Marcellinus where the audience of the musician consists of sheep only. This conception of Christ is found in Christian literary works in which Orpheus appears as an early teacher of religious rites, and as a revealer of the one true God, as well as a charmer of wild animals. We are here concerned with the last-mentioned function, which is recognized as a foreshadowing of the work of Christ in taming the wicked souls of men. It is most natural that this similarity should have occurred to Christians who had any knowledge of mythology. The most notable picture of Christ/Orpheus is in Domitilla, where he is thronged by sundry animals.

The pictures of the shepherd milking a sheep require little comment. Sometimes he is carrying a pail of milk, food for the babes in Christ, to whom St Paul, the Epistle to the Hebrews, and I Peter refer (I Cor. 3.1–2, Heb. 5–12, I Peter 2.2). The provision of milk by the Shepherd is mentioned by Perpetua in the vision that she saw when in prison before her martyrdom (*Acta* 4); St Augustine refers to this in a sermon *De tempore barbarico*, in which he says that the provision of this milk inspired Perpetua in her sufferings.

There is one picture, in Domitilla, where a serpent, striped   75
black and white, is coiled round a tree close to a sheep which does not appear to be scared by its somewhat aggressive presence. This picture is unique, and its interpretation may be that the serpent, i.e. Satan, is now powerless to harm his erstwhile victims. Wilpert (p. 425) regarded the picture as based on Psalm 90.13. The sheep in the picture could be regarded as treading on the serpent's tail.

The scene from St John's Gospel of the encounter of Jesus with the woman of Samaria at Jacob's well is found on five occasions   76
in various catacombs (cf. p. 84, above). Since it embodies some of the most sublime teaching of our Lord, this scene is not unsuited to a catacomb setting. As we have shown when discussing those depicting miracles, such scenes are intimately connected with the revelation of Jesus as messiah, which is central to the meeting at the well; to reinforce the appositeness of the scene, we have also the teaching about the well of water springing up to eternal life. (This picture is also found in the baptistery at Dura.

75 *Domitilla*. The sheep
and the serpent

76 *Via Latina*. Jesus and
the woman of Samaria at
Jacob's well (but cf. p. 84)

77 *Via Latina*. The
sermon on the mount (cf.
Ill. 87)

78 Peter and Marcellinus.
The man with the book

79 *Domitilla*. The martyr Petronella introduces Veneranda to paradise. Note the open book and the box for books to right

This scene can naturally lead us on to representations of Christ teaching, as exemplified by the 'Sermon on the Mount'. There is an explicit example of this at the Via Latina (but cf. p. 84, above), and at the Viale Manzoni there is a picture that shows Christ seated on a mountain with an open scroll in his hands while below him is his flock of sheep.

But catacomb art afforded little scope for reproduction of pictures from parables or discourses, even if they were apposite. Of the former we have only the wise virgins with their torches raised, from the *Coemeterium Maius*, who are about to partake of a banquet represented on the left-hand side of the same *arcosolium*. Both wise and foolish are seen in a picture from Cyriaca. The importance of this parable in the Christian scheme of life and death is shown by references to the lot of the wise virgins in various liturgies.

Even though the teaching mission of Christ does not particularly reveal itself in the catacombs, it was not forgotten that Christianity was a religion of a book. 'What have you in your case?' said the proconsul to the accused Speratus in Africa in AD 180, 'The Books, and the letters of a just man, one Paul' was the reply. Boxes of books appear over and over again, e.g. in the

78

80 *Commodilla*. The denial of Peter

picture in Domitilla of the reception of Veneranda into paradise and in the mosaic in the same catacomb (Ills. 79, 92), and reference will be made below to such boxes in the scenes of judgement with which we shall shortly deal. The teacher with his disciples appears on reliefs on sarcophagi. In Peter and Marcellinus, and at the Via Latina, a man is seen holding a book.

The paucity of reference to Christ's trial, death and resurrection has already been noted. Christians were not unmindful of these events, and on sarcophagi we find reliefs of the denial of Peter and of Pilate's hand-washing. The former is twice found in catacomb art, at Cyriaca and Commodilla. The significance of the scheme in Cyriaca, where it appears on the tomb of a consecrated virgin(!) has been variously estimated. Garruchi thought of it as a warning not to trust in oneself, de Rossi as a reference to the future faith of Peter. Wilpert thought that it referred to the fact that *all* are under sin. But there is little more. In Praetextatus we have the scene of Jesus crowned with thorns at the moment represented in Mark 15.19, 'They struck his head with a reed' (cf. Matt. 27.30).

A picture at the Via Latina is supposed to represent the casting of lots for the garments of Jesus. The scene with its large urn for

80

81

82

81 *Praetextatus.* The crown of thorns. The scene represents Mk 15.19 'They struck his head with a reed.'

82 *Via Latina.* Right-hand side of painting, which shows the soldiers casting lots for the tunic of Jesus. A soldier is seen turning the jar in which the lots were placed. But for another possible interpretation see p. 101

reception of the lots is unnatural compared to the simple statement in the gospels of something done – more or less on the spur of the moment – immediately after the Crucifixion. But why this scene should have attracted attention even in a catacomb with such a varied repertoire of pictures we cannot tell. Goodenough thought this interpretation interesting and possible, but not at all convincing, and that the picture could equally well refer to the scene in I Samuel 14.41–2 in which Saul and Jonathan cast the oracular Urim and Thummim, to decide on which of them guilt for sin rested.

We have seen how the fact of the Resurrection was established indirectly but firmly. We lack examples of representations of this momentous happening, though at Dura we have a picture of the women at the tomb. But the relationship of Christ to the believers was not ended. 'Just as it is appointed for men to die once, and after that comes judgement' (Heb. 9.27), we must all appear before the judgement seat of Christ (2 Cor. 5.10). So the

83 *Coemeterium Maius.* Christ as judge. Note the boxes of books

judgement and its sequel are subjects very suited to the art of the catacombs.

Wilpert listed fourteen examples of such scenes. The identification of the pictures has not passed unchallenged, and it has been suggested that scenes of ordination or of teaching may be represented. But even so it is difficult to regard such pictures as depicting anything other than what happens to the Christian 83 after death. At its simplest the scene represents Christ seated alone, but clearly in a position of authority, but other obvious figures are those of the 'accused', in the attitude of an *orans*, of saints acting as advocates of the accused, of sheep typifying the elect flock. Another feature is the boxes of books. In the judgement scenes of the *Book of Revelation*, the books are most important, and the inclusion of one's name in the Lamb's Book of Life. 'I saw the dead, great and small, standing before the throne, and books were opened . . . And the dead were judged by what was written in the books, by what they had done' (Rev. 20.12).

There is no place in catacomb art for judgement or condemnation. Christ gives his followers a favourable judgement. While in the thought of the early Christians the idea of hell for the wicked is a certainty (cf. p. 155), those who appear in the catacomb paintings are acquitted. 'There is no place', as Faber wrote in his hymn, 'where earth's failings have such kindly judgement given.'

It remains only to show how the Lord was portrayed in heavenly majesty. As examples of this we may mention the picture in Peter and Marcellinus, described above (pp. 59–60), 32 where the Lord appears between the Apostles Peter and Paul, while below are the four saints with whom the catacomb was connected, and the Lamb standing on Mount Zion, from which the rivers of paradise flow. Similarly, both in Commodilla and at the Via Latina, there is a picture of the majestic Christ. This is the latest kind of picture that belongs to the period in which the catacombs were in use. Last of all we reach the 'statuesque' pictures of the sixth and seventh centuries placed in underground basilicas, or in other spots frequented by visitors.

Such then is the Christian's pilgrimage. 'The great contribution of catacomb art is to show us a faith much simpler and more direct than the faith of the involved theologians of the time.'[50]

The Burial Places of Heretics and Schismatics

What have heretics to do with Christians?

Tertullian.

From our literary sources one would deduce that Rome was swarming with heretics and schismatics in the early centuries. It is quite clear that the City attracted teachers and doctrines of various sorts, and the number of Christian teachers who came to Rome permanently or temporarily was large, particularly in the second and early third centuries. A great deal of theological controversy had, if not its beginnings, its centre in Rome.

Heretics and schismatics, like others, had to die and be buried, and it is to be expected that, in the vast extent and variety of the catacombs, some traces would survive of the burial places of Marcionites, Montanists, Monarchians (of whatever sort), and Novatianists, to mention only a few. It is therefore a matter of interest to see whether we can identify their sepulchres, and to extend the enquiry to consider whether syncretists also, and even straight pagans were ever buried in Christian catacombs. Severanus, the continuator of Bosio, has already been mentioned as most unwilling to admit any contamination of Christian cemeteries; Misson and Bishop Burnet on the other hand (p. 52, above) are unwilling to admit the fundamentally Christian character of the catacombs at all!

Now, heretical burial places *are* found in and around Rome, but if we were to add up the total areas of these the space available for burial would not fulfil the expectations as to numbers aroused by the literary sources. In two cases only, the catacombs of Hippolytus and Novatian, do we find large burial places, and these are associated with schismatics rather than with heretics. The catacomb of Hippolytus near the Via Tiburtina was identified from his statue found there which gives him the character of a bishop seated in his *cathedra*. There is nothing else to distinguish this catacomb from any other, and moreover the

84 The tomb of Novatian. NOVATIANO BEATISSIMO MARTURI GAUDENTIUS DIAC. F(ECIT). This inscription is *in situ* in the catacomb of Novatian

schism of Hippolytus was of brief duration and soon forgotten. We have already seen (p. 37, above) how the tomb of the martyr Hippolytus attracted throngs of visitors in the late fourth century. What the association of Hippolytus and his statue with the catacombs shows is that by about 230 a schismatic Christian body possessed wealth enough to own a considerable property.

The sect of Novatianists is however far more important. Their founder Novatian was the most prominent of the Roman presbyters around the year 250, but he went into schism because of the rigorous views that he sponsored in dealing with those who had 'lapsed' in the persecution under Decius, and because of his own failure to be elected bishop when persecution ended. Nevertheless, he secured consecration, in a 'hole and corner' way as an opposition bishop, and his followers continued to exist as a strict but dissenting body till at any rate the fifth century. They spread to Constantinople, to Asia, and to other parts of the East in the fourth century, where they enjoyed a measure of toleration, and even the friendship of bishops of the Eastern capital. It may also be recalled that their special position was recognized by Constantine, who included a Novatianist bishop among those invited to the Council of Nicaea. But their situation worsened in the early fifth century when at Rome and Constantinople they were repressed by Bishops Coelestine (422–32) and Nestorius (428–31). It was a matter of intense interest when a new catacomb was discovered in 1926–32 near the junction of the Via Tiburtina and the modern Viale Regina Marghareta. It is not mentioned in any of the *Itineraries* or by any explorer of the catacombs. In the last-mentioned year there was found a tomb with the inscription 'For the blessed martyr Novatian Gaudentius the deacon made [this tomb].' Now Socrates, the fifth-century Church historian, who gives us much information about the Novatianists, says that Novatian was a martyr in the persecution under Valerian (258). The tomb itself is not large enough to hold a body, so relics must have been

84

deposited there, and this may indicate that Novatian died in exile. The identity of the martyr and the schismatic cannot be absolutely established, but the tomb appears to date from *c.* 270–300. The relics were probably removed from the tomb at a later date and deposited in the church built above. In any case the catacomb appears to have been abandoned in the fifth century, which corresponds to the period in which Coelestine repressed the sect.

The *Hypogaeum* on the Viale Manzoni has already been mentioned. It was discovered in 1919, and has a special interest in that its situation, inside the Aurelian walls, shows that it is anterior to these, a circumstance confirmed by the discovery that bricks used in its construction indicate that this part of it at any rate was built in the time of the Severi. It can scarcely be called a catacomb, consisting as it does of several rooms at varying levels, though there are traces of an adjacent development of passages, which could have been the beginnings of one. All in all, its construction was pursued over quite a lengthy period of time. There can be no doubt that the *Hypogaeum* is Christian.

If we consider the state of affairs in the early third century, we must remember that the situation was very different from the one that we see today. The digging of catacombs was still in its beginnings, and in itself the *Hypogaeum* must have appeared not as a burial place insignificant in size compared to the vast extent of the catacombs as they later existed, but as challenging

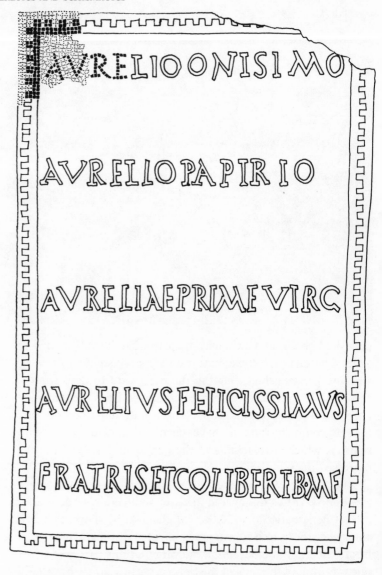

86 *Viale Manzoni*. The
Mosaic of the Aurelii

comparison with them. It was used by Christians who demanded

85 elaborate painted decoration in their burial place, and who felt
no repugnance to the use of, say, a picture from classical
mythology.

The first notable feature is a mosaic inscription which

86 AURELIUS FELICISSIMUS, a freedman, set there in
memory of three other AURELII, his brothers and fellow
freedmen. (One of the three so described is in fact a woman,
AURELIA PRIMA, who is characterized as VIRGO.) Here
therefore is a burial place belonging to a group, just as at St
Sebastian there is the tomb of the INNOCENTIORES, for it is

87 *Viale Manzoni*. The shepherd, who in the words of the inscription of Avircius Marcellus (*c.* AD 180) 'feeds the flocks of sheep on mountains and plains'. Here, with his scroll, he is also represented as a teacher

far more likely that the word FRATRIS (FRATRIBUS) refers to members of a group rather than to members of one family. These AURELII took their name from the imperial family, just as did AURELIUS, a priest of Mithras, buried in the catacomb of Vibia (p. 122, below).

The rooms contain *arcosolia*, and further tombs were dug in the floors. The walls and ceilings are richly decorated. There is a great deal of purely decorative art, but in actual pictures there are some unusual features. There is for instance a scene representing the creation of the first man by the demiurgus to which reference is made elsewhere (see p. 65, above). this feature may (but need not) reflect Gnostic influence. Various other pictures would be perfectly in place in a 'catholic' catacomb, e.g. the shepherd on the mountain with his flock (? including goats), a picture which, as Cecchelli points out,[51] has a distinct resemblance to the shepherd described in the inscription of Avircius; the same also applies to a banquet scene. What is more unusual are pictures of groups of figures (? initiates or apostles). The quality of painting in some of these figures is among the finest in catacomb art.

But much more unusual is the representation of the return of Ulysses, the scene of the triumphant horseman entering a city, and that of the man who points to the cross. These pictures have been the subject of ingenious conjecture as to their meaning. In the case of the first-named there is surely too much of the story of Ulysses obvious in it to admit of any doubt as to the subject. Two scenes are depicted, one above the other. In the lower scene we see, to the right, Ulysses, still a beggar, then Penelope and her web on the loom, to the left of which are three suitors, nude figures advancing proudly (in conformity to their character in the Homeric narrative). In the upper scene are the buildings of the palace, and a large herd of sheep and goats (which, in Homer, the suitors were despoiling). Now, in the *Philosophoumena* (*Refutation of all heresies*) of Hippolytus (VI 13) Ulysses is compared to Christ in his resistance to the enticement of the Sirens' song. In our picture he returns to claim his patrimony and his bride (the Church) and to destroy the proud. The Homeric story was already deeply inwrought into Christian literary works, a circumstance which we can see particularly in Clement of Alexandria. Homer too, as Hippolytus tells us, was particularly the prophet of a sect called the Naassenes, but there is no need to connect them with this picture. Hippolytus, to be sure, gives a great deal of information about them (V 7–8) and they may have appeared in Rome.

Then there are the pictures showing a conqueror riding into a city in triumph, awaited by a group of persons, and a city, in a square or courtyard of which someone on a lofty seat is presiding over, teaching or judging a crowd. To the former of these, varied interpretations have been given: that it represents the triumph of Anti-Christ,[52] or of Hercules, or of Epiphanes, son of the Alexandrian Carpocrates, to whom a temple had been erected at Samé in Cephallenia, the birthplace of his mother, where 'the islanders used to gather once a month for a religious beano in celebration of their hero's birthday'.[53] But, as an alternative to these, the victor is surely Christ entering the Holy City, not now

Opposite
88 *Viale Manzoni.* Group of apostles or initiates.

89 *Viale Manzoni.* The return of Ulysses. There are two pictures, one above the other

87

88

89

90, 91

90 *Viale Manzoni*. The conqueror entering the city. He can be seen on horseback to the left of the delegation waiting at the gate

91 *Viale Manzoni*. The heavenly Jerusalem. The gate is guarded by an angel, and within the courtyard a multitude is being taught or judged

'lowly and riding on an ass' (Zech. 9.9), but claiming his rule; the ass, to be sure, appears in the picture in a stall: it is now no longer necessary. He too is the judge or teacher on the lofty seat. Finally, there is the picture of the man who points to the cross. The sign of the cross is rare in catacomb art, but not unknown, and really calls for no special comment.

It cannot be said that the suggestions made about the identity of the sectaries of the Viale Manzoni lead us anywhere; so one more may do no harm. In the early third century Christian doctrine was still at a formative stage, as the arguments between the bishops Zephyrinus and Callistus on the one hand, and the presbyter (pseudo-bishop) Hippolytus on the other, show. There was one sect, the 'dynamic' Monarchians, who were in Rome at this time – not an extensive group, but probably wealthy and appreciative of philosophic tradition. 'To study Euclid is for some of them a labour of love; Aristotle and Theophrastus are admired', says an opponent, probably Hippolytus. But this is the merest suggestion; such sentiments were not theirs alone: according to Irenaeus, the Carpocratians honoured pictures of Pythagoras, Plato and Aristotle (see also p. 61, above). But the well-known licentiousness of the Carpocratians would ill accord with the designation of Aurelia Prima as VIRGO!

As the Monarchians have just been mentioned, without explanation, it is necessary to indicate briefly what their views were. Their Christianity must be regarded as utterly genuine, but attached to a theology which the main body of Christians rejected. They were deeply concerned for the unity, the sole rule, the *monarchia* of God, that appeared to be threatened by the theology of the *Logos* or Word, which prevailed in much Christian writing in the second century. The relation of the Word to God was undefined and could lead to the idea that the Christians were not monotheists, but worshipped two Gods. The Monarchians offered two different solutions of the problem. the 'Dynamic' Monarchians, referred to above, taught that Jesus was a man upon whom the power (*dunamis*) of God came down at his baptism: he was 'adopted' as Son. The 'Modalist' Monarchians held that the one God existed in three different 'modes', Father, Son and Spirit, and that therefore, at the incarnation, the fullness of the Godhead descended, called by the name of the Son. The Modalists were by far the more important. Their thought remained active for centuries, often called Sabellianism, from Sabellius, one of its chief advocates, who was active in Rome in the early years of the third century. They existed still in Rome in the fourth century, and a mosaic in an *arcosolium* of the catacomb of Domitilla may bear witness to their presence. This mosaic was seen by Marangoni in 1742, and rediscovered in the present century. The mosaic represents Christ seated between Peter and Paul: in front of them is a box for documents, such as is 92 seen elsewhere in other pictures. But the accompanying inscription is interesting, QUI ET FILIUS DICERIS ET PATER INVENIRIS, 'Thou who art called the Son, are also found (to be) the Father.' This inscription is Sabellian. Its date is fourth century, as is shown by the appearance of the Chi-rho monogram, and it may be from about the period of Damasus, bishop from 366 to 384.

Under St Sebastian on the Via Appia Antica there are three 93 tombs on a *piazzuola*. These were originally surface tombs, cut

92 *Domitilla*. Mosaic in an *arcosolium*, showing Christ seated between Peter and Paul. The *arcosolium* carries the inscription (not visible in the photograph) QUI ET FILIUS DICERIS ET PATER INUENIRIS. The mosaic dates to the middle or late fourth century

93 The three tombs under the basilica of St Sebastian. To right, that of M. Clodius Hermes, and in the centre that of the INNOCENTIORES, a guild or club. The date of the latter is mid-third century. The tombs were completely buried in the reconstruction that took place in the third century

M CLODIVS HERMES

into the side of a former *arenarium*. The right-hand tomb, that of M. CLODIUS HERMES, had pictures above its gabled entrance which have now disappeared. Among these were four banquet scenes, where the participants at each table number five. Food was on the tables before them, but its nature was not easily distinguishable. To the left a flock was grazing and a 'good shepherd' appeared above them carrying a sheep, while at the extreme left a figure stretched out his arms towards the shepherd. There were two groups of figures at centre and right, and a group of three at the extreme right. These pictures are not now extant (cf. Ill. 93 with Ill. 94), and no attempt will be made to elucidate them. In the interior of the tomb there are no specifically Christian paintings, only scenes that may be said to approach Christianity. There are remains of a burial of ashes after incineration, which was overtaken by the change to inhumation (? late in the second century). The central tomb of the three is the sepulchre of the INNOCENTIORES, a guild or club, who have left inscriptions of about the date 240. In this tomb there is a *graffito* of a fish, which may indicate Christian infiltration. The third tomb has a decoration of vine branches,

94 *St Sebastian*. Scenes once represented above the lintel of the door of the tomb of M. Clodius Hermes. The tomb was originally pagan or syncretist. To left, flock of sheep with 'Good Shepherd' to whom another figure gesticulates. In centre and far right, two groups of persons; right of centre, four banquet scenes with from five to eight (only five according to Cecchelli) persons in each. These pictures have now vanished

93

119

95 *Vibia*. The judgement of Vibia in the underworld of classical mythology. Enthroned on the judges' tribunal are Pluto (Dispater) and Persephone (Aeracura)

96 *Vibia*. There are two scenes here. To left, Vibia, granted a favourable judgement is led by a (?her) good angel into the banquet of the blessed, seen to right. Vibia is the third of the six persons at table

which Cecchelli[54] regarded as similar to that of the Crypt of the Flavians in Domitilla. But all this ended in the late third century, when the *piazzuola* was filled in, as has already been mentioned (p. 32, above).

The small catacomb of Vibia on the Via Appia Antica nearly opposite the catacomb of Callistus is undoubtedly syncretistic. The process of death, judgement, and reception of Vibia, wife of Vincentius, a priest of (Jupiter) Sabazius, is revealed in such detail as it not found in any specifically Christian scene of judgement. For instance the names of individual figures are

97 *Vibia*. The banquet of
the 'seven pious priests',
adjoining the pictures
dealing with Vibia.
Among the priests is
Vincentius, Vibia's
husband

placed beside or above them, a feature not generally found. We
see Vibia carried off by Pluto to the world below (ABREPTIO
VIBIES), in a way very similar to the story of Persephone in the
myth; Mercury (i.e. Hermes, the conductor of souls) stands
ready to conduct her on her journey (DISCENSIO) below, and
she is then brought to the *tribunal* (judgement seat) of
DISPATER (Pluto) and AERACURA (Persephone – Juno
Stygia). She is accompanied by Mercury (MERCURIUS
NUNTIUS) who carries his *caduceus* (staff) in his left hand, and
a wand in his right. Vibia is accompanied by Alcestis, the type of
a faithful wife, and to the left of the tribunal stand the three Fates
(FATA DIVINA), the goddesses of Destiny. All was well,
however, and Vibia is next shown being led through the gate
(INDUCTIO VIBIES) by a (? her) good angel (ANGELUS
BONUS) to a feast where she sits third from the left among the
six participants, men and women. These have been judged
worthy in the judgement of the good (BONORUM IUDICIO
IUDICATI) to have the banquet, which is taking place in a
garden. There are four servants, and the food is fish, bread and
wine. At the side of the *arcosolium* there is another banquet scene
where SEPTEM PII SACERDOTES, one of whom is
Vincentius, are seated. Their food consists of bread marked with
a cross, fish, cake,[55] and a hare or rabbit. Vincentius, as an
inscription above the *arcosolium* shows, was a priest of (Jupiter)
SABAZIUS. So were, we may assume, all the seven priests. The

95

96

97

inscription may be translated as follows: '[The tomb] of Vincentius: what thou beholdest is the gate of rest. Many have gone before me, I await all. Eat, drink, play and come to me. When thou livest, do good, this thou shalt carry with thee. Vincentius, priest of the god Sabazius. This [is] he who served the holy rites of the gods with pious mind.'

Near by are two other *acrosolia*, one containing pictures that belong to some mystery cult that cannot now be designated, and the other the funeral inscription of Aurelius, a priest of Mithras. Among these indications of paganism evidence of Christian burials is not wanting. The burials that we have mentioned all appear to belong to the last stages of the catacomb's use. The floor of the gallery concerned had twice been lowered to make more room, and the date appears to be towards the end of the fourth century. Perhaps this contiguity of the older religions and the new shows us that progress from one to the other was not a uniform process, that religious influences in families varied during the fourth century, and that backsliding occurred.

Of all heretical sects the Montanists, called after their founder Montanus, were one of the most ubiquitous. They originated in Phrygia soon after the middle of the second century, but had reached Rome, and even the remote churches of the Rhône valley, before its end. They were distinguished from every other sort of heretic by the fact that many of them diverged from the Catholics in only one particular, though indeed an important one, namely in the continued open manifestation of the works of the spirit in new prophecies. At Rome their early emissaries had even a certain success with the bishop (? Victor), who was restrained from giving the sect his approval only by the (? opportune) arrival from Asia of one Praxeas, who clarified the situation in the East, showing that the Montanists were deluded, or impostors who foisted their new prophetic teaching on a Church in which 'prophets' were not now of first importance, in which there was an almost fixed canon of Christian scripture, and in which a regular and well-ordered hierarchy was the guardian and propagator of traditional teaching derived from the Apostles. But Montanism had its attractions for ardent spirits, as is shown by the conversion of Tertullian at Carthage.

Roman documents do not fail to mention them. Hippolytus, about 220, states that some Montanists had followed Monarchian error, and the 'Muratorian fragment', a document of *c.* 190, that gives an account of what the Roman Church believed about Christian scripture, rejects them. Moreover there existed the text of a dialogue between Gaius, a Roman Christian, and Proclus, a Montanist, a fragment of which contains the famous reference to the 'trophies' of the Apostles at the Vatican and on the Ostian road.

We find traces of Montanist possession of, or infiltration into, burial places. They are candidates for possession of the *Hypogaeum* of the Viale Manzoni, but this attribution really lacks sound foundation. There are, however, definite indications to connect persons from Asia, who may be Montanists, with the catacomb of St Pancras, under the church of that dedication in Trastevere. A later source describes the martyr Pancras himself as being originally from Phrygia. An inscription recorded by Boldetti, but now lost, mentions ABLABES (Lat. *innocens*), who was a Galatian and a 'spiritual' man (*pneumaticos*). Other inscriptions refer to Galatians connected with this cemetery, including Philip, son of a presbyter Alypius.

98 *Pancras*. The inscription for Botrys, a Christian

In the same cemetery there is an inscription for BOTRYS, a Christian. Such a mention of 'a Christian' is, for Rome, 'of exceptional rarity',[56] and the *loculi* of the *cubiculum* concerned, from peculiarities in their structure, may preserve traces of Asian funerary architecture. Another inscription from St Paul-outside-the-Walls refers to a 'Christian' named Sozomen. There was no need to apply the term to a Christian buried among Christians unless there was some special reason. More striking is the inscription of the physician Alexander, found 'in the area beyond the Tiber', who is both Christian and *pneumaticos*. The name Alexander is one that occurs significantly in Asian circles, and the title 'Christian' is a feature of Montanist inscriptions in Asia Minor. But it must also be noted that the term 'Christian' is quite frequent in Sicilian inscriptions, where Montanist influence need not be postulated.

For the fourth century, the great period of the catacombs, we lack evidence (but cf. p. 117, above); yet the question of the burial of dissident groups must still have been with the Church. Concerning the Donatist schismatics, emigrants from Africa, we find that they worshipped in a cave outside the city, shielded by a fence of wicker-work. But whether this was a burial place as well as a place of worship we cannot tell. Anyhow, if we may believe Optatus, the anti-Donatist writer (assuredly not an unprejudiced witness), they amounted to a mere handful of persons.

It may be noted finally that in the East, Emperor Leo I, by an edict of 457, ordered heretics, 'since we have considered it to be humane and holy', to be buried with the customary burial rites.

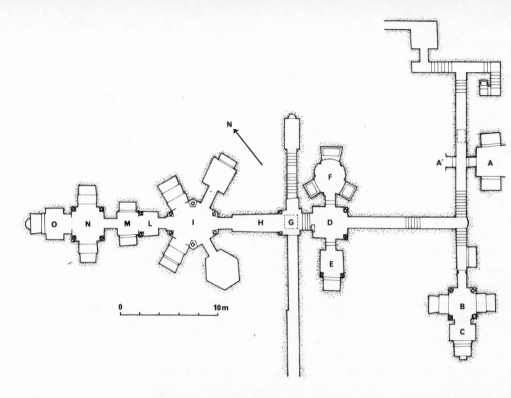

99 *Via Latina*. Plan of the catacomb

The edict does not say 'in the customary burial places', but perhaps that may be assumed, as the edict may have been issued under the influence of the barbarian patrician Aspar, himself an Arian, through whose influence Leo had been made Emperor. But in any case this is not evidence about what was going on in Rome or the West.

Besides the pictures that adorn the burial places of heretics and schismatics, there is, as has already been pointed out, a great deal of decoration that has nothing to do with Christianity. Leaving aside the elements that are purely decorative, and figures such as Cupid and Psyche, Oceanus, the seasons, and *putti*, which show how close Christian and pagan modes of decoration were to each other, we shall now consider various pictures that appear in a Christian setting, but that are of scenes and figures derived from Greek mythology, which Christians were supposed to abhor. The pictures concerned come from the 99 catacomb at the Via Latina, and from their prominence there it is obvious that these subjects could not have been unacceptable to those in charge. It has already been noted that this catacomb was no ordinary one, but probably belonged to a circle of wealthy families. Either these families were made up of both Christians and pagans and did not eschew the fact of being buried together, or, if they were entirely Christian, they felt no repugnance to the classical stories. Perhaps the pictures indicate that in certain circles relations between adherents of the old and the new religions were far more friendly than our literary sources admit, or that Christians found in the old stories material not inconsistent with their faith.

Of these pictures the most striking are connected with Hercules, who, denigrated among others by Lactantius in the early fourth century on account of his violence and moral turpitude, eventually was the subject of 'une christianisation totale'.[57] The attitude of Lactantius is one that we would expect to find, as the recent severe persecution was conducted in part by rulers of the Herculian dynasty. But enlightened pagan thought had, long before the fourth century AD, passed far beyond the idea that Hercules was a mere drunkard or glutton. He was a man who in a life of toil had purged the earth of monsters, and eventually was received as a god in Olympus. Long before the Christian era, Hercules was regarded as having chosen the way of virtue rather than that of vice.

100 *Via Latina.* The return of Alcestis. Note the elaborate decoration of the ceiling

The pictures of Hercules occur in one *cubiculum* only, that labelled N on the accompanying plan. We see the dying Admetus, who was to be saved from death by the self-sacrifice of
100 his wife Alcestis, surrounded by his family. Another picture shows Alcestis being led back from Hades by Hercules, and presented to her husband. The artist has caused Hercules to make good use of his journey to Hades, for he has brought up Cerberus as well, on a single visit! He, like Christ, descended into hell on a mission of rescue. With regard to Alcestis we have already seen how she stood as a patron of Vibia (p. 121, above) at her judgement before the gods of the underworld.

The other pictures representing Hercules show two of his
101 'labours', a meeting of Hercules with Minerva (Athena), and Hercules killing an enemy. The labours portrayed are the killing of the Lernaean hydra, and the winning of the apples of the Hesperides. In the former the hero, armed only with his club, must have found it a hard task to dispose of the many-headed reptile; in the latter the artist has forgotten that it was Atlas who secured the apples notwithstanding the formidable serpent which guarded them, while Hercules upheld the world in his stead. The two pictures each lead to the death or deluding of the serpent. Then there are pictures of Hercules killing an enemy (? Antaeus), and exchanging greetings with Athena (Minerva), the goddess of arts and wisdom, i.e. the union of virtue and learning. This is not our sole evidence of the meeting of these two: a gold-glass medallion with this scene was illustrated by F. Buonarotti in 1716 in his work on gold-glass fragments found in Roman cemeteries, but the present whereabouts of this medallion is unknown. Moreover, the contest of Hercules and Antaeus, with Minerva as spectator, appears on a floor mosaic from Bramdean in Hampshire, and similar scenes have been mentioned above in the tomb of the Statilii (p. 58).

102 In *cubiculum* E a picture represents the death of Cleopatra, and is the only one there that admits of identification. It is impossible to tell now why the death of the Egyptian queen was illustrated. Other interpretations have indeed been suggested – the union of Jupiter with Proserpine, which produced Dionysius Sabazius, and which was symbolically enacted in the mysteries of that cult; or the union of Olympias, queen of Macedonia, with a serpent, from which according to the story Alexander the Great was born. As the figure of 'Cleopatra' has a *nimbus* it is clear that she is a queen or a goddess, and a third suggestion that she may be the mother of Plato, visited by Apollo, may be discounted. Egyptian

101 *Via Latina*. The death of Cleopatra

102 *Via Latina*. The meeting of Minerva and Hercules (see p. 58)

103 *Via Latina*. The anatomy lesson (see p. 84)

103

104 *(opposite) Priscilla.*
The Phoenix, as a symbol of resurrection

influence on the pictures in this catacomb, particularly that of Samson killing the lion, has been suggested. There is also a picture of an Egyptian soldier (connected with the passage of the Red Sea by the Israelites).

A similar difficulty of interpretation occurs with the 'anatomy lesson' of *cubiculum* I. This scene is also without parallel in extant pictures. A group of seated persons, under the guidance or tutelage of one predominant figure, clad only in a *pallium*, or philosopher's cloak, is occupied in the examination of a human body, the interior of whose abdomen is open to view. Whether

the body be alive or dead it is hard to tell. One of the group holds a wand or pointer with which he indicates the body. The instructor may represent a famous doctor buried there, and additional similar figures portrayed on near-by panels of roof or walls may indicate others of the same profession. While the idea of a lesson in anatomy or surgery has the greatest verisimilitude, it must be mentioned that the picture has been thought to represent a scene of resurrection, a miraculous cure, the fate of Judas Iscariot (Acts 1.18), or the creation of the first man by God, in the presence of the angels. But certainty is impossible.

Before leaving the catacomb of the Via Latina, it should perhaps be noted that, as can be seen on the plan, the final graves beyond *cubicula* C and O block the passages and impede further development. The burial in O reached after passing the pictures described above, is indubitably Christian.

In the catacombs of Priscilla and Callistus are notable examples of the mingling of Christian and pagan ideas in the 104 portrayal of the Phoenix, the mythical bird of the East, as a symbol of resurrection. This creature, at the end of its life of 500 years, immolated itself on a pyre, and from the flames a new Phoenix issued. The Phoenix is mentioned as a symbol of resurrection by Clement of Rome, *c.* AD 96, and was the subject of the sole surviving poem of Lactantius, written *c.* AD 300.

8

Sicily, Tunisia, Naples, Malta

There is no speech, nor are there words, their voice is not heard, yet their voice goes out through all the earth, and their words to the ends of the world.

Psalm 19, 3–4, R.S.V.

It has already been pointed out that there are catacombs in many other places besides Rome. Numerous small catacombs are found in Italy, and at one site, Naples, there exists the vast catacomb of San Gennaro, which, with lesser cemeteries in the vicinity, shows that Christians were swarming in that area around AD 400. Beyond Italy the main sites are in Sicily, Malta and Tunisia.

The remains of paintings, compared with what exists at Rome are not extensive, except at Naples: the same applies to inscriptions, except in Sicily. We can gain little information about the spread of Christianity, any more than we can of the day to day existence of the inhabitants of the Empire outside the capital. For in this respect the general history is shrouded in obscurity; for example, J. Führer and V. Schultze, in their fundamental study of Christian cemeteries in Sicily,[58] refer to 'the darkness into which Sicily sinks under Roman domination'. But they describe no fewer than 23 sites (or areas) in the island, which show how important Christianity became.

If we consider these catacombs in general terms we can see in some places identity or similarity in construction with those at Rome, in others differences, even fundamental differences. Of the 'Roman' type one may cite the catacombs of Syracuse and Palermo in Sicily, and at Sousse (Hadrumetum) in North Africa. But in the rest of Sicily, in Malta, and, less definitely, in Naples, long galleries, with *loculi* and *arcosolia* in the walls are absent. The graves are grouped in much smaller areas and are most frequently of the *baldacchino* type that is almost unknown at Rome, particularly in Sicily and Malta, and large open spaces are found that would be suitable for gatherings of Christians.

105 *Baldacchino* tombs at Larderia, Sicily

The *baldacchino* is formed of pillars of natural rock left untouched when the tombs were hollowed out and reaching to the ceiling. Such graves are also sometimes fenced off or protected by a *transenna* (cf. p. 139), 'a kind of marble or stone grille', with numerous perforations arranged in simple rows. These *transennae* mark the graves of more important persons but are not necessarily those of martyrs. Another feature of Sicilian catacombs is a form of *arcosolium* whose arch is much larger than those we have already studied, and in which the space for burials is extended inwards, often for a considerable distance, so that graves numbering up to twenty or even more can be placed behind one another.

106

Now, the catacombs in which the graves are grouped and in which there are no long passages are continuing a type of burial place that had existed in Sicily and Malta (not to mention Sardinia and South Italy) for several millennia. For example, the extrances to rock-cut tombs at Cava Lazzaro and at Castelluccio in south-east Sicily[59] are just like the initial stages of some Christian catacombs in Malta. The terrain enabled tombs to be constructed very near the surface, and inhabitants of Sicily and Malta went on fashioning the same type of burial place century after century. There are in general no passages, though an example of incipient development may be seen in Malta in 'the

106 Syracuse. Vigna
Cassia, one of the large
arcosolia containing a
number of graves, one
behind the other

enormous and elaborately constructed and decorated *hypogaeum* at Hal Saflieni'.[60]

The early history of Christianity in Sicily, so far as literary sources are concerned, is almost non-existent. St Paul stayed three days at Syracuse on his journey from Malta to Rome (Acts 28.12), but it is hazardous to assume that his brief visit has any real significance for the development of Sicilian Christianity. In the mid-third century Cyprian once mentions Christianity in Sicily, and in 314 Chraestus, Bishop of Syracuse, was invited to the Council of Arles by Constantine. The history of Sicilian Christianity, in so far as it exists, does so in the vast extent of its burial places, and in the surviving inscriptions. In this respect de Rossi called Syracuse the *sorella minore* of Rome. But Constantine's invitation to Chraestus surely points to a well established Christian community, which must have arisen many years previously.

At Syracuse the main sepulchral area lies north of the 'island' of Ortygia, towards the slopes of Achadrina, an area once included in the city, but which eventually, owing to a dwindling population, lay outside it. The main catacombs are those of St Lucy, who has already been mentioned as a martyr in the persecution under Diocletian and is the patron saint of the city (p. 37), of San Giovanni, and of the Vigna Cassia and Santa

107

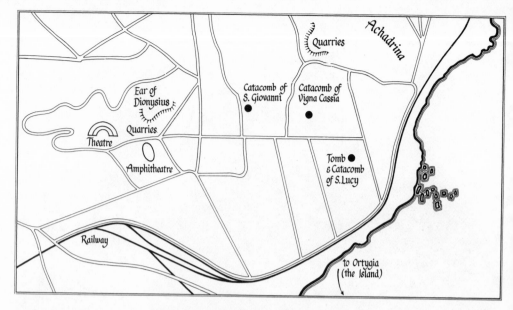

107 Syracuse. The catacomb area

Maria di Gesù, the two last-named being contiguous. There are numerous individual tombs as well. In particular, mention may be made of Sepulchre Street (Strada dei Sepolcri), behind the theatre, with its hollowed-out rock tombs, constructed in an age when the theatre must have been past its heyday as a place for stage performances.

108   Of the catacombs named above, that of the Vigna Cassia is probably the earliest, originally formed by the linking of smaller *hypogaea* and going back, if we may place reliance on the dates of coins found in it, to the third century. As can be seen from Führer's plan, this catacomb, and the contiguous one of Santa

108   Maria di Gesù, have in them all types of structure: the open space, perhaps a scene of the cult of some martyr, passages lined with *loculi* (some of these passages are among the loftiest with as many as 14 *loculi* above one another), round water cisterns incorporated into the plan, as in other places also, and finally a large area of *arcosolia*-type tombs with the graves behind one another. There are few *cubicula*. Notwithstanding the closeness of these catacombs to each other they are connected only by a water channel.

Opposite

108 (*above*) Syracuse. Plan of the catacomb of the Vigna Cassia and of Santa Maria di Gesù

109 (*below*) Syracuse. Plan of the catacomb of San Giovanni

The catacomb of St Lucy is associated with the tomb of the saint, which is enshrined in a modern building though her relics were removed many centuries ago. She was, as has already been noted, a martyr in the persecution under Diocletian, but the Christian occupation of part at any rate of the catacomb probably goes back to the third century. Here too we can, as it were, see the

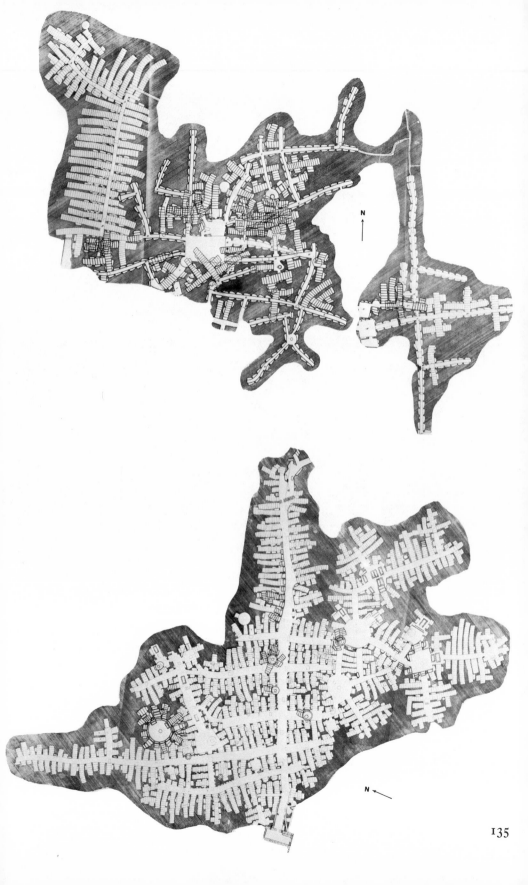

110 Syracuse. Vigna Cassia. Floral decoration

111 Syracuse. Vigna Cassia, a eucharistic scene (?)

Christian occupation in progress, as in its course it overwhelmed a pagan shrine of which the painted human figures, taking part in some cult act, were mutilated by the devotees of the new religion. There have also been found votive offerings, *idoletti*, in small trenches in the floor, and there are niches in which sepulchral urns were placed.

109   But of all the Syracusan catacombs that of San Giovanni is the most striking, owing to the immensity of its structure and the size of its passages. It gives the impression of a project undertaken by a Church that had an assured position and had no

need of concealment. A large passage, from which other wide passages branch off at right angles, crosses the whole site. This passage was, to be sure, originally a water-conduit, but as we have already seen, the Christians did not eschew such adventitious aids in the construction of burial places. Another noteworthy feature is the large circular rotundas, with burials in walls and floor, in one of which was found the sarcophagus of Adelfia. Many later burials must have been destructive of paintings and other decoration. This catacomb also is not without its martyr traditions. Near its entrance is the crypt of St Marcian at the site where a martyr of that name, reputedly an early bishop of Syracuse, suffered, and the close contiguity of catacomb and shrine may be an indication that Christian burials began in this area in the pre-Constantinian period.

As it is at Syracuse that nearly all the remains of paintings are found, it will not be inapposite to mention them at this point. In one of his works[61] G. Agnello illustrates 36 pictures of varying importance, all of which come from Syracuse, with the exception of six which belong to one other site, Marsala. The subjects are, in general, the same as we have found in Rome: *orantes*, the Shepherd, Daniel, Jonah, Mary and her Child, the Eucharist and the reception of a Christian, after death, by Christ.

We shall particularize about two only of the most noteworthy paintings, both from the Vigna Cassia. First, there is a 'eucharistic' scene in an *arcosolium*, in which is seen to the left the figure of a girl (an *orans*), and to the right a seated male personage of quite enormous build, richly robed, and holding in his right hand a cup. This figure is unlike anything found in catacomb painting, and can well be called, as Agnello does, *Lo strano personaggio*.[62] We cannot determine whether the scene represents the giving of Holy Communion in this world, or a banquet in heaven.

Secondly, there is the best preserved of all Syracusan paintings, the presentation to Christ of Marcia. We have already considered similar scenes found at Rome, and the present one does not really differ from these. At the right of the picture Marcia, who, as an inscription says, lived 25 years, 8 months and 15 days, kneels before Christ and the Apostles Peter and Paul, stretching out her right hand in supplication. Christ extends his right hand towards her in a gesture of welcome and a further inscription adds 'Remember Thy servant Marcia'. Below the *arcosolium* two peacocks, birds dear to Syracusan painters, flank a vase, symbol of the *refrigerium* of the soul (pp. 163–5, below). In

111

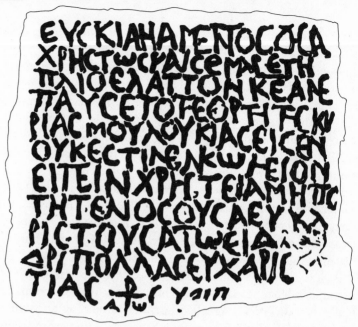

112 Syracuse. San Giovanni. The inscription of Euskia. 'Euskia the blameless. She lived a good and holy life of about twenty-five years. She died on the festival day of my lady Lucia. It is not possible to give Euskia sufficient praise. She was a Christian, faithful and perfect, a sharer often in mutual joy with her very own husband.' (The last phrase is hard to translate, but it indicates, as Agnello says, 'un delicato ricordo all' affeto maritale'.)

the catacomb of San Giovanni there is a similar scene, much damaged, of the crowning of the virgin Deodata. This picture has the additional interest that it is a palimpsest, substituted for an original version, and the *graffiti* of pilgrims may indicate that Deodata was regarded as a martyr. The two paintings that have been described show scenes that take place in gardens of flowers and plants, and with them, in this respect, we may compare Ill. 110, where an *arcosolium* and contiguous walls (also in the Vigna Cassia), are almost smothered in floral decoration. The 'normal' catacomb pictures of, for example, Jonah and Daniel are also present, and indicate that the Christians of Syracuse were subject to the same preoccupations as were those at Rome.

The site of Acrae (Palazzolo-Acreide) about 20 miles west of Syracuse, is full of interest. This city was a colony of Syracuse founded in 664 BC, designed to protect the mother city against inroads from the interior. The ancient city has practically disappeared, apart from the theatre and the remains of an adjacent council chamber. But burial places remain, excavated in the sides of two large stone-quarries. In the course of the fourth and fifth centuries AD Acrae established itself as the most important Christian centre of eastern Sicily after Syracuse. 'The many large catacombs of the city itself and of its adjacent territory . . . and the numerous Christian inscriptions testify to this.'[63] Most of the graves are of the *baldacchino* type, fashioned in groups with short passages dividing one group from another.

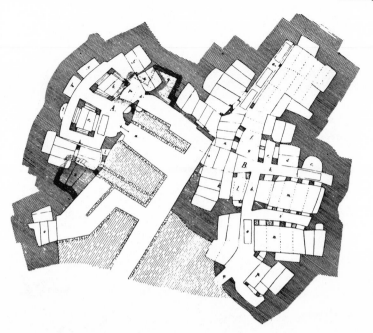

113 Acrae. Plan of the
catacomb of Intagliata

These cemeteries are now called *Intagliata* and *Intagliatella*. In
the latter a room contains rows of adjacent graves on the floor,
with sides three or four feet high. Some tombs are fenced off by
transennae (p. 132). These are surely the tombs of more important
people, but not necessarily of martyrs. No paintings, and only a
few inscriptions have survived. The origin and development of
these quarries goes far back beyond the Christian era and they
were, well before that, being used for burials or for votive
plaques and inscriptions to which the numerous niches in the
rocky walls bear witness. The countryside around is full of
tombs, great and small, and among these the Grotto of
Sennebardo, a short distance south-west of the theatre,
challenges comparison, in size, with the two catacombs that have
just been mentioned. The dates of these, to judge from coins
found in them, ranges from the third to the fifth century.

At Agrigento, near the Temple of Concord, there is an
extensive Christian cemetery above ground, and also a catacomb
of considerable size. This catacomb, called Grotta Fragapani, is
very near the surface, and its main passage (B in Ill. 114) may
always have been open to the sky, as it is today. The makers of
this catacomb used existing water cisterns to aid their work.
There are three circular rotundas, but these are smaller than the
ones at San Giovanni at Syracuse. Traces of painted decoration
can be recognized. This cemetery, again, must date from the
third to the fifth century. As elsewhere there are numerous other

114

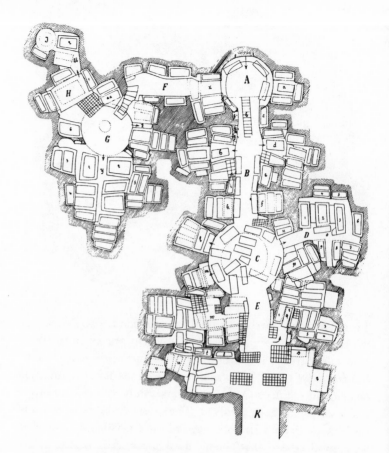

114 Agrigento. Plan of the catacomb of Fragapani. Note rotundas, the largest of which (C) has numerous graves in the floor

tombs near by, some of them in the form of *arcosolia* built into the city walls. The Christians at Agrigento took over a large pagan cemetery, but the date of this take-over, and also the question of whether the said cemetery had already been abandoned, cannot be certainly answered.

At Lilybaeum-Marsala, in the far west of the island, there are several catacombs. This city was described by Cicero[64] as *splendidissima civitas*: its present-day name, Marsala, belongs to the period of the Saracens. It was at Lilybaeum that the Neoplatonist philosopher Porphyry wrote his famous work *Against the Christians* in the late third century. Its Christian traditions' go back to the second century. The Church of Lilybaeum attained to a certain importance in the fifth century, when Bishop Paschasinus was a trusted agent of Pope Leo the Great. The catacombs of Marsala are notable for the richness of their floral and linear decoration. The only picture of the Good Shepherd as yet found in Sicily, outside Syracuse, came from

Marsala, but it was destroyed towards the end of the last century, in the construction of a modern cemetery. A painting of it exists in the Museum at Palermo.

The early history of Christianity in Palermo is, as elsewhere in Sicily, shrouded in obscurity. But cemeteries are to be found, notably the large catacomb of the Porta Ossuna, which was discovered in the eighteenth century. In general this follows the pattern of Sicilian cemeteries, i.e. the *arcosolia* have graves placed one behind the other. Immediately inside the entrance there is an open space which holds what may have been an *agape* table, similar to those that will be mentioned in connection with the catacombs of Malta (p. 148, below). No other catacomb is so lacking in actual Christian remains; so much so, that it has even been supposed that the structure is not Christian but Phoenician! However, general probability indicates that it is the former.

The Christian antiquities of Sicily have been investigated by, among others, the German scholars J. Führer and V. Schultze, and by the Italian P. Orsi, who for many years was indefatigable in his explorations. In more recent times their work has been continued, particularly by G. and S.-L. Agnello.

The most notable catacombs in North Africa are at Sousse (Hadrumetum) in Tunisia. Their exploration owes most to A. F. Leynaud, afterwards Archbishop of Algiers, but it had its beginnings in excavations made under the guidance of officers in the French Army from 1885 onwards. The terrain at Sousse was, in some measure, admirably suited to the digging of catacombs (though it should be pointed out that the North African Christians constructed large cemeteries on the surface and that catacombs are not the rule). But at Sousse a thin layer of soil had below it a hard stratum of travertine stone, which could form a ceiling to the excavations, made in tufa immediately below. The Christian catacombs are three in number, named from monuments or inscriptions found in them the catacomb of the Good Shepherd, of Hermes, and of Severus. There is also a pagan catacomb, of Agrippa, smaller than the above-mentioned Christian ones, but indicating how in some cases pagans might construct catacombs. From objects found it appears to have been in use from *c.* 230 to the beginning of the fourth century. One inscription is for a little slave girl DIIS MANIBUS/SACRIS PULA (i.e. puella) VER/NALIA NOMINE/PERPETUA VIXIT ANNIS/DECE MENSES TRES/ORAS OCTO, 'To the holy gods below: Perpetua, a slave girl; she lived ten years, three months, eight hours.' In so far as they have been explored, the catacombs of Sousse contain 13,000 or more burials, but their full extent is difficult to assess. The passages are low, with space for not more than four *loculi* above one another, and there are few *cubicula*. The bodies of the dead were frequently placed in *loculi* on a layer of fresh plaster, and covered with a sheath of the same substance. Hence, when *loculi* have been opened, the outline of part of the body can be seen, as though it had been in a mould. The bones have perished. It is clear also that older galleries were filled with the débris from more recent excavations to an even greater extent than at Rome.

Christianity was taking hold at Hadrumetum probably by the end of the second century. We know this, for instance, from the reference in Tertullian to the martyrdom of Maiulus or Mavilus, which took place in the amphitheatre there on 12 May 212; from the correspondence of Cyprian, moreover, we learn that the city had a bishop, Polycarp, at the middle of the third century. But we know nothing of this Church that bears on the controversies about the lapsed, about the re-baptism of heretics, or, in the fourth century, about Manichaeism or Donatism.

The progress from the old to the new religion is not unmarked. For instance there is the tomb of the 'Epicurean' Eustorgius, who had inscribed on his grave his seven precepts: EUSTORGIUS DICIT, etc. e.g. BIBITE IUVENES DUM POSSETIS (i.e. POTESTIS) BIBERE. Two of the precepts mention God, one of which reads DEUS ODIT UXORE(M) MALI MORI(S) A(C) FILIU(M) IN ALOGIA ET USURA, 'God hates a wife of ill morals, and a son plunged in senselessness and debt.' Eustorgius praises his wife in almost fulsome terms – she is RARISSIMA UNICA FILOSOFA, she is also MIRI EXEMPLI ET PUDORIS. But the wife's tomb also has the Christian IN PACE, and a Constantinian monogram found its way on to the tomb of Eustorgius himself, while an immediately contiguous grave bears the unmistakably Christian name of COTBULDEUS (i.e. Quodvultdeus). Here is a family in process of becoming Christian. The *Tabularius* (archivist) Successus left a similar tribute to his wife Eusebia, INNOCUA VERE CONIUNX EXEMPLI RARISSIMI SEXUS: on the last three words Foucher drily remarks, 'L'expression pourrait laisser assez peu d'illusions sur la vertu des Hadrumétines'.[65]

The inscriptions from the catacombs of North Africa are not numerous enough to enable conclusions to be drawn from them about the Christians of Hadrumetum. Several, besides those

115

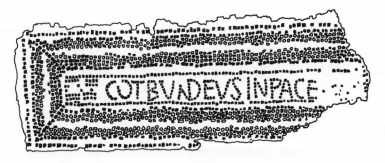

115 Sousse. Funeral
mosaic of Cotbuldeus
(Quodvultdeus)

116 Sousse. Funeral
mosaic of a child, Renata

already mentioned are interesting: the Greek inscription of
Parthenope for instance, an immigrant from Smyrna (fourth
century) or of Claudius Chraestus, *vir egregius et praeses*. As
might be expected in a land noted for the number and excellence
of its mosaics, Christians often placed mosaics on the graves,
frequently on those of children. The examples illustrated here   116
are now in the Museum. In the Catacomb of Hermes was found
the grave of Arisus, the shortest-lived of all those commemorated anywhere. The inscription reads ARISUS IN
PACE/NATUS ORA SEXTA/BIXIT SS VIII, implying that
he lived for a few moments only.

It is clear that there were Christians at Puteoli and Pompeii,
on the Campanian coast, in the first century. Evidence for
Naples in that period is lacking, but we may assume that in the
second century the new religion was taking a firm hold there.
The earliest remains of Christian paintings are dated by H.
Achelis to the second century.[66] These are ceiling paintings, and,
like those in the Crypt of the Flavians in Rome (p. 58), show no
specifically Christian features. There are sea-horses, deer, birds
and plants, and human heads and figures. But continuing from
these the Neapolitan catacombs exhibit a series of paintings
extending to about the tenth century, a feature to which further
reference will be made.

117 Naples. Entrance to the upper level of the catacomb of San Gennaro

The catacombs of Naples have already been mentioned (p. 52) in connection with the travels of Bishop Burnet. It is no wonder that he found them notable when he compared them with those at Rome. For the catacomb of San Gennaro can justly be compared only with that of San Giovanni at Syracuse. All the extant Neapolitan catacombs are in the area called Capodimonte, but only that of San Gennaro is important; the others, five in number, contribute a few notable paintings, but add little to our general information.

117   In its present form on two levels the catacomb of San Gennaro belongs to the fourth century. But before this time, smaller Christian tombs existed in the area which, as in other places, were linked to form one large catacomb. This is undoubtedly the case with what is now the vestibule of the lower catacomb, originally designed to contain six graves only. It was much altered when the area ceased to be a family tomb, and really became a vestibule from which proceed two long and wide passages leading through the catacomb. In the eighth century it became a baptistery. The relics of St Januarius were brought to

Naples in the fifth century by Bishop John I (d. 432) and eventually found their resting place in this catacomb; where they may have displaced the memory of a 'confessor' Agrippinus, an earlier bishop of Naples. It appears however that John built an oratory for the relics, and was himself buried there. This Januarius has no connection with the martyr of that name interred in the catacomb of Praetextatus in Rome. He became the patron saint of Naples, and to the present day has been linked to the Church there by the closest ties. The Neapolitan saint is probably to be identified with the bishop of Beneventum who was present at the (Western) Council of Sardica in 343. We do not know how he gained the title of martyr in the tangled doctrinal controversies of the fourth century. Echoes (probably faint ones) of these may be heard in the attendance at the Eastern Council of Sardica of Fortunatus of Naples; that is, he adhered to the 'pro-Arian' faction, and thus has disappeared from the list of bishops of Naples, perhaps because he was sent into exile by the Western emperor Constans, who was a staunch Nicene. In view of Greek influences both mercantile and perhaps doctrinal on Naples, the position of Fortunatus is not surprising. As Achelis points out,[67] however, the situation is not quite so simple as this, as in another document connected with the Council of Sardica, one Calepodius appears as bishop of Naples. Two rival claimants may have been disputing the see, but there we must leave the question and return to the catacombs.

The two levels of the catacomb of San Gennaro are adjacent, but not directly above each other, and the wide open spaces in both of these are most noteworthy. The walls are lined with *arcosolia* and *loculi*; there are also numerous *cubicula*, and passages leading into other areas. As in Sicily, graves are sometimes placed, in *arcosolia*, one behind the other, but not to the number found at Syracuse, and in general, *cubicula* are open to the main passages across their whole width. There is only one tomb of a *baldacchino* type. During the centuries a great deal of rebuilding was done which destroyed numerous primitive features: in particular a crypt for the burial of bishops may be   26 mentioned, constructed perhaps in imitation of the papal crypt at Rome.

This catacomb remained in use as a burial place for longer than those of Rome and was used in periods of plague even in modern times. The picture, now much damaged, that is unique in early Christian art, is derived from the *Shepherd* of Hermas, a work that has already been mentioned (p. 56), and which was, in

118 Naples. *Arcosolium* of Cominia and (the child) Nicatiola, with St Januarius and lighted candles between them

some places regarded as scripture. We have a scene showing three girls assisting in building the tower (i.e. the Church). They are sturdy maidens who appear to be handling blocks of stone with ease. It is interesting to note that in the *Shepherd*, Hermas shows a certain knowledge of near-by Cumae. As the importance of the book, considered as scripture, receded, the presence of this picture would be an additional indication of a date in the third century. From this century onwards we find the usual pictures: the decoration of ceilings with animals and plants, the Fall, Noah; Moses (Peter) striking the rock, Jonah, Daniel, Christ (with the Apostles) and Christ (alone) carrying his wonder-working staff, and *orantes*. From the fifth century onwards the biblical subjects vanish, and the connexion of the Neapolitan pictures with the art of the Roman catacombs comes to an end. Instead we have pictures containing 'portraits' of saints and of the individuals buried in the tombs, often accompanied by lighted candles. This may be connected with the fact that in 536 Naples became part of the Byzantine Empire and remained so until the eighth century.

118

The saints portrayed are in the first place those of universal import, Peter and Paul in particular. An interesting picture from the fifth century (at San Severo, not at San Gennaro) is that of the Milanese saint Protasius (perhaps originally accompanied by his comrade Gervasius) whose relics were discovered by Ambrose at Milan in 386. We can see how the cult of these new

146

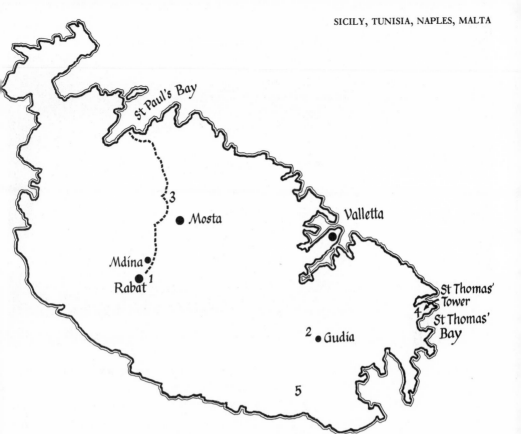

saints spread. We know from Paulinus of Nola (d. 431) that it had reached Campania in the early fifth century. At the same time, we may note that Severus, bishop of Naples, was a friend of St Ambrose, to whom the latter addressed a letter in AD 393.

The Church of Naples, so far as we know, produced no martyrs of its own. Nor did the Church of Malta. But Agatha, martyred at Catania, was supposed to have spent some time in hiding on the island when pursued by an importunate suitor. In Malta, as at Syracuse, we may begin with the lengthy stay of St Paul throughout a winter after his shipwreck on the island. It is hard to believe that the Apostle kept silence during so long a stay. But once again it is impossible to detect any impact that he may have made on the inhabitants.

In 1530 Philip de l'Isle Adam, Grand Master of the Knights of Malta, granted a request to two persons that they be allowed to search for hidden treasure on the island, with the stipulation that one third of their finds should go to the Order and the Church. What this permission meant was that the cemeteries of Malta were systematically plundered and the effects of this campaign can be seen in their present-day condition.

119 Malta. Map of the island

KEY

1 Catacombs of St Paul, St Agatha, Abbatia-Tad-Deyr

2 Rock tomb near Gudia

3 The 'Tal Bistra' catacombs near road from Rabat to St Paul's Bay

4 Catacomb near St Thomas' Tower

5 Entrance to country catacomb (see Ill. 126)

120 Malta. St Paul's catacombs, Rabat. Canopied tombs

The Christian cemeteries on the island go back in origin to the types of tombs made by pre-Christian inhabitants: these are small tomb chambers hollowed out in the rock, and the use of such tombs by Christians continued during the period in which more extensive catacombs were being constructed. Actual catacombs are, in general, those in the vicinity of Mdina, the ancient capital.

120   The Maltese catacombs have certain features that are peculiar to themselves. There are proportionately far fewer *loculi* than elsewhere; there are a large number of canopied or *baldacchino* tombs, similar to those in Sicily. The majority of these tombs are for two bodies; head-rests were inserted at one end, and the bodies were placed in the tomb through, as it were, a window. The shape of the 'lid', which is carved out of rock and is not separate, has given the name 'saddle-backed' to these tombs.

121   We have already had occasion to mention (pp. 19, 96–7) commemorative meals held at the tombs of martyrs or of deceased relatives. In Malta there are, even in small catacombs, circular structures fashioned in the floor, to which the name
123   '*agape* tables' has been given, and round which the participants in such celebrations must have reclined. They are so common in Malta that they represent a distinctive feature of Maltese Christianity. It is not that such 'tables' are unknown elsewhere. Becker [68] shows examples from Pompeii (pagan, of course) and North Africa, and a further example may exist at Palermo (p. 140 above). The Maltese catacombs have yielded few inscriptions, and only the most meagre remains of paintings.

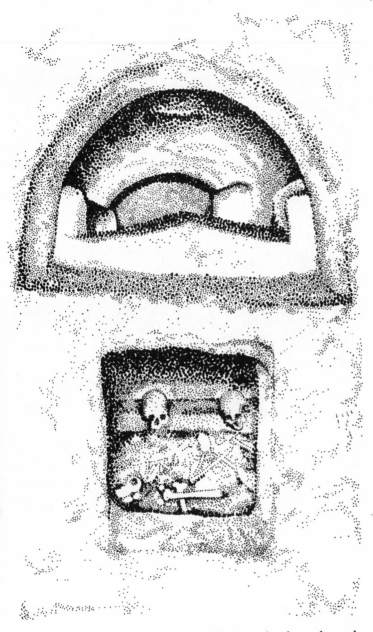

121 Malta. St Paul's
catacombs, Rabat.
'Saddle-backed' tomb,
with the 'window' through
which bodies were
inserted

Besides the larger catacombs, small ones exist throughout the island, of which three of the more interesting will be mentioned here. Accounts of two of them were given by Sir T. Zammit and by Dr C. G. Zammit.[69] At Hal-Resqun, a small catacomb containing four graves was discovered in 1887. There is also a ruined *agape* table, and an attempt (abandoned) to construct another grave chamber. But the chief interest lies in the somewhat rudely carved reliefs. One of these, the naming of the   36

122 Malta. Differing floor
levels in St Paul's
catacombs

123 Malta. '*Agape* table'
in St Paul's catacombs

animals at the Creation, has already been mentioned. The other is of two pelicans feeding their young, a symbolic representation of the sacrifice of Christ, as 'the pelican was always supposed to be in the habit of feeding its young with the flesh and blood of its own breast'.[70] 124

The second of these small catacombs is constructed under a rocky ledge, at the edge of a plateau called Tal-Bistra, near the 125 road leading from Rabat to St Paul's Bay. The frontage of this catacomb extends for more than one hundred yards and is constructed on the same basis as that at Abbatia Tad-Deyr. But in the course of centuries the outer portion has been destroyed, so that what remains does not penetrate into the rock more than about ten yards. There are numerous entrances across the whole frontage, one of which is illustrated here. The whole catacomb has been completely plundered, and finds made in it are minimal.

Finally, there is a small catacomb near Fort St Thomas, which contains a biblical inscription based on Acts 3.6 and on Psalm 3.7 or 118.25, or on Matthew 14.30. The first portion reads, 'In the name of Jesus Christ rise and walk,' the second, 'Lord, make me whole'.

As mentioned earlier, the Maltese catacombs, properly speaking, are in the vicinity of Mdina, the ancient capital. The town of Rabat, just outside the walls of Mdina, is in fact largely built on catacombs, which form the cellars of modern houses. The three main groups are St Paul's, St Agatha's and Abbatia Tad-Deyr; of these St Paul's, impressive for its spaciousness and for its canopied or *baldacchino* tombs, is the group most visited. The complex associated with the name of St Agatha and also that of Abbatia Tad-Deyr are interesting for the fact that in both are found representations of the seven-branched candlestick. This 127 shows either that these were Jewish, or that in certain circumstances Jews and Christians did not live in constant mutual hostility, or that there was a strong Jewish influence on Maltese Christianity. There is also some decoration in relief in the form of shell or whorl patterns and of tools of trade. Sometimes tomb chambers are closed by heavy stone doors just 128 as prehistoric tombs in Malta sometimes were. The general impression left by the Maltese catacombs is that they derive their form from Sicily more than from any other source. It is most probable that they belong to the fourth–sixth centuries, those of Tad-Deyr being the latest, as they are farther away from the centres of population.

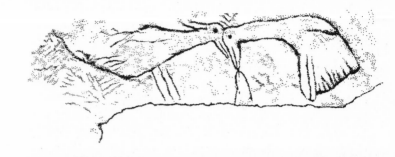

124 Malta. Hal-Resqun:
pelicans feeding their
young

125 Malta. Tal-Bistra:
one of the entrances to the
catacomb

126 Malta. Entrance to a
country catacomb (5 on
map, Ill. 119)

127 Malta. Seven-
branched candlestick

128 Malta. Burial
chamber closed by stone
door

9
The Life and Death of the Christians

Not many . . . wise . . . not many . . . powerful, not many of noble birth

1 Cor. 1.26

The *Cappella Greca* in the catacomb of Priscilla has been mentioned several times. While it is notable for the pictures of the *fractio panis* and of the story of Susanna (pp. 80–1, 94) the *Cappella* gained its name from two Greek inscriptions painted on the plaster, memorials placed there by Obrimus (towards the beginning of the third century) in memory of his cousin Palladius and his own wife Nestoriana. The inscription for Palladius is indeed 'for remembrance' sake', *Mnemes charin*, and Nestoriana is called 'blessed', *macaria*: both are called sweetest, *glucucatoi*. There was yet another tie with Palladius; he was *synscholastes*, a fellow student, and in this context, perhaps that means 'a fellow Christian'. We may assume, from the position of the inscriptions that Obrimus was an important person among the Roman Christians, and that at a time when Greek was the prevailing language among them. But, like so much else in the early history of Christianity, nothing survives to tell us anything about Obrimus and the others.

These two inscriptions are seen, if not remarked, by more visitors than any others in the catacombs. But even in their simplicity they convey more than the vast majority of inscriptions, the brevity of which has already been noticed (p. 61, above). Yet they do not contain the commonest phrase of all, IN PACE (EN EIRENE(I)). The expectation of peace is stated in utter confidence; it amounts to a certainty, as is found in Psalm 4.8, 'In peace I will both lie down and sleep', or chapter 3 of the *Wisdom of Solomon* where, after tribulation, the souls of the righteous are at peace, ILLI AUTEM SUNT IN PACE (3.3) (cf. p. 61). Above all, peace was what the Lord had promised to his followers (Jn 14.27). In St Augustine's view the believer could not know true peace in this world, which was denied him

129

OBPIMOCΠAΛΛΑΔIω
ΓΛΥΚΥΤΑΤω ΑΝΕΨΙω
CΥΝCΧΟΛΛCΤ HMNHMHC
XAPIN

OBPIMOC·NECTOPIANH
MAKAPIAΓΛΥΚΥΤΑTH

129 *Priscilla*. The inscriptions set up by Obrimus

by the devil, by heretics, by schismatics, by the world in general
and by himself. He enjoys true peace in eternity alone, peace that
was not however something passive and inactive. The dead were
ultimately connected with the living, for, when the latter passed
from this world they were intensely in need of the active
intercession of those who had gone before them, namely, of the
Virgin (cf. p. 88, above), of the Apostles, of the martyrs and
saints. Conversely, the prayers of the dead were necessary for the
living. IN MENTE NOS ABETO PARENTES TUOS.[71] That
is as far as 'catacomb religion' goes. There is little about the end
of the world, and the final judgement. We have already seen (p.
108, above) how the dead appear before Christ as judge, and the
favourable judgement that he gives. But from Christian
literature of the early centuries we must conclude that
punishment for the wicked is a certainty. That can perhaps be
further elucidated from our next point.

We shall begin with the story in St Luke of the rich man and
the beggar (16.19ff.). There is no doubt that the condition of
each of the two in the next world is exactly opposite, the one
being in Hades in torment, the other in Abraham's bosom. The
rich man asked the beggar to 'refresh' his tongue with water. The
word *refrigero* and its noun *refrigerium* occur frequently in
Christian literature and in inscriptions. They indicate total bliss
in refreshment, than which no greater joy can be conceived. A
reference to the refreshment to be found with Abraham, Isaac and
Jacob is exemplified in an inscription from San Giovanni at
Syracuse, 'Remember, O God, Thy servant Chrysis, and grant
her a shining land (to dwell in), a place of refreshment
(*anapsyxis*) in the bosoms of Abraham, Isaac and Jacob'.[72] But
before we discuss the *refrigerium* further, let us consider the
people who were to experience it.

The number of pictures and inscriptions that refer to earthly
circumstances is small, compared with the mass of material that
exists. Wilpert pointed out[73] long ago how few the relevant
pictures are; in fact he enumerated five examples only. (1) In the
Coemeterium Maius there is a picture of a man with a wagon,
drawn by oxen, and loaded with a barrel. That may be a real
indication of the earthly métier of the person buried there. (2) In
Priscilla there is the 'crypt of the coopers': eight men are
standing by two large barrels, and these may be members of a
collegium, who were buried in that part of the cemetery. (3) In
Domitilla there is a picture, unfortunately much damaged, of a
seller of vegetables, standing by a table on which her goods are

displayed. (4) In Pontian we can see the transport of oil by boat. (5) An area in Domitilla has obvious reference to the landing of grain and the work of bakers. This catacomb was not far distant from the quays on the Tiber where grain was landed, and it would not be unnatural for Christian members of the *corpus caudic-ariorum*, who manned the vessels employed in bringing the grain up the river from Ostia, and for members of the *corpus pistorum*, the guild of bakers, to be buried there.

About the end of the second century, Tertullian laid it down in his work *On Idolatry*, that certain occupations were not allowed to Christians. These prohibitions, while perhaps strictly logical, certainly limited the life that Christians could live in the world. Some of them, as early as the time of Tertullian, were inclined towards compromise, even to the extent that a maker of idols might be found in Holy Orders.[74] It would not be natural for such a one, if a Christian, to proclaim his occupation on his

Opposite

130 (*above*) *Priscilla*. The crypt of the coopers

131 (*below*) *Domitilla*. The transport of grain: to left, the ramp from the ship

132 *Peter and Marcellinus.* The gladiator

133 *Peter and Marcellinus.*
The dancer

134 *Praetextatus.* The
surgeon's implements

tomb, but as time went on, things changed: Wilpert identified [75] in the catacombs the graves of a soldier and of a charioteer, dating as we might expect, from the fourth century. Another instance of Christians as soldiers occurs in the case of the two martyrs Achilleus and Nereus (p. 28, above). Even more striking than these is the picture in Peter and Marcellinus of a gladiator, a *retiarius*, with his net thrown over his shoulder. This may be construed as a sign of spiritual struggle, but why should this be so in an age when Christianity was spreading in all classes? Similarly, in the same catacomb, there is a picture of a dancer, more 'covered' than the bevy of fourth-century dancers at Piazza Armerina in Sicily, but a dancer none the less. As a symbol of joy, the image of dancing is common in the Old Testament, e.g. in

133

135 Malta. Relief showing tools (cf. Ill. 134)

136 The fishmonger(?)

137 *Marcus and Marcellianus*. The shop

IVLIVSMARIVSSILVANVS
ETIVLIAMARTINAVVI
FECFRVNTSIBIVTIN
DEOVIVANT

Psalms 149.3, 150.4, or, more particularly, in Jeremiah 31.4, 'Then shall the maidens rejoice in the dance', a passage in which the prophet proclaims the return of God's people from exile, and its general blessedness.

Other ways in which professions or occupations are revealed are the sets of instruments or tools set in relief on graves, such as the surgeon's tools or the smith's (from Malta), both here illustrated. We possess too a relief of a maker of sarcophagi at work, and a fishmonger in his shop; but in the latter case, in the uncertainty that surrounds so much of this kind of study, the relief has been construed as preparation for a sacred meal, in which, as we have seen, fish was one of the particular constituents.

134–137

159

The connexion of Christianity with learning grew closer as time went on. That this religion was the religion of a book must have become obvious, and a book requires exposition. Hence the idea that Christianity was a philosophy grew common even in the second century – an idea not confined to Christians only – and became exemplified in the highly educated Christians of Alexandria like Clement and Origen. A religion that included teaching on morality was far more akin to a philosophy than to the general run of ancient religion (if we except some mystery cults of limited appeal). So we find the man with a book, and sometimes his disciples. We have already seen Christ as teacher, and reliefs of the teacher and pupils are found, more on *sarcophagi* than in paintings. But we have seen the importance of books in several pictures (Ills 79, 83, 92), and Illustration 78 shows a picture of a man with a book. This kind of portrayal would be very natural in the fourth century when most Christians had come to terms with inherited pagan education.

78

Record of other occupations is found. Some of them[76] are a locksmith (*clabarius* [sic], a linen weaver (*lintearius*), a seller of barley 'from the Via Nova', a 'cloak-room' attendant (*capsarius*) from the Baths of Caracalla, while in St Callistus there is the inscription of Dionysius, doctor and presbyter – but a mere list must be avoided.

Sometimes we find in the catacombs scenes, as distinct from decoration, that are without religious significance. For instance in the catacomb of the Jordani there is a hunting scene, with animals in headlong flight, and similar pictures come from the catacomb of the 'Hunters'. Christians of all generations have taken pleasure in the chase: in antiquity we may remember the emperor Gratian, Synesius, bishop of Ptolemais (Cyrene), and the Gallic nobles of the fifth century. There is also a hunting scene on the lid of an undoubtedly Christian sarcophagus at St Sebastian, but that, of course, might have been bought already carved from the shop. On the other hand, the catacomb of Trebius Justus contains scenes of everyday life that have no connexion with Christianity at all. They portray active elements of country life, and of great possessions. With regard to the latter, one may compare the epitaph of Callistratus, a wealthy Christian of Carthage, who made no secret of the fact that he had great possessions,[77] except that the tomb of Trebius Justus can be construed as not being a Christian one.

138

139

Now we must pass on to references in inscriptions to more human relationships. The inscriptions, brief as they are,

138 *Jordani*. A hunting scene

sometimes contain a word or words that show feeling in the relationship of dead and living. Husbands and wives lived 'without discord', children can be called 'dearest', 'innocent', a husband can be called 'incomparable', and we have already illustrated the inscription of Euskia at Syracuse. A child is called AGNUS SINE MACULA, 'a lamb without stain'.

112

The coming of the Christian Empire in the fourth century meant that the attitude of the Christians towards the State and its offices was completely altered. They were no longer insignificant politically though for many a day the emperors had to go on employing pagans as well. Even before the fourth century, however, women of senatorial rank were wives of persons of lower status. The following is from the catacomb of Callistus:[78]

AELIUS SATURNINUS
CASSIE(ae) FARETRIAE CLARISSIME (ae)
FEMINE(ae) CONIUGI BENEME
RENTI DEPOSITIO TERTU NO
NAS FEBRARIAS

The wife of Aelius Saturninus was a woman of senatorial rank, *Clarissima Femina* (CF in brief), and on this inscription Josi adds, 'This is one of the typical examples of those marriages between ladies of senatorial rank and persons of lower status, according to the regulation of Pope Callistus.' Unfortunately,

139 (*opposite*) The tomb of Trebius Justus

140 *Pamphilus*. Inscription in crude mosaic, 'Martyrs, holy, good and blessed help Quiracus'

once more we know nothing of the persons concerned, nor of those in other similar inscriptions, which might throw light on the effect of the marriage rules for Christians instituted by Callistus.

One effect of the changed status of Christians is that inscriptions become longer, and are written in verse.

But beyond all earthly position and title ranked the appellation MARTYR. The tombs of the witnesses who had sacrificed all were places of especial veneration. We have already had occasion to comment on this (p. 37, above), and to note that this title was applied to the bishops of Rome buried in the Papal Crypt.

'Martyrs, holy, good, blessed, help Quiriacus' runs an inscription in crude mosaic in the catacomb of Pamphilus. There 140
was a great desire to be buried near martyrs and this desire, and also the multitudes of pilgrims who visited their tombs led to alterations in the lay-out of adjacent areas. Their intercessions for the living were particularly sought. MARTYRES SANCTI IN MENTE HAUITE (habete) MARIA(m) is part of one inscription.

The pilgrims were inveterate scribblers of *graffiti* at these sites, e.g. at the tomb of Callistus in the catacomb of Calepodius, at the tomb of Sixtus II in or near the Papal Crypt in Callistus, and most strikingly of all at the site *ad Catacumbas*. As has 18
already been noted, visitors there left many *graffiti* calling on the Apostles. Thus, PETRE ED(et) PAULE SUBVENITE PRIM(itivo) PECCATORI, 'help Primitivus a sinner'; PAULAE (*sic* = PAULE ET) PETRE IN ORATIONES B(v)OST(ras) NOS IN MENTAE (*sic*) (H)ABETE ET PLURES, 'Paul and Peter have us in mind in your prayers, and more than us'. These numerous appeals to the Apostles must be actively connected with the *refrigerium*. At its simplest, the *refrigerium*

141 *Priscilla*. Does this inscription mark the grave of a martyr Vericundus?

142 Funeral inscription of Severa

143 Funeral inscription of Firmia Victora, with a ship sailing in past the lighthouse (at Ostia?)

can be experienced in this world as the solace brought to the poor in an actual meal:[79] it can next be extended to a meal provided by a Christian for others. An inscription from Priscilla tells how, in the year 375 certain persons came there AD CALICEM, i.e. to drink. And at *ad Catacumbas* we find XIII KAL APRILES REFRIGERAVI PARTHENIUS IN DEO ET NOS IN DEO OMNES, 'On 20 March I, Parthenius, took my refreshment in God, as we all did'. Such celebrations might degenerate into orgies, 'very like the superstitious practices of the heathen', as Augustine said, but many Christians must have enjoyed them. Here are three examples:[80]

JANUARIA BENE REFRIGERA ET ROGA PRO NOS

REFRIGERATUR ANIMA

ANTONIA, DULCIS ANIMA, IN PACE TIBI
REFRIGERIT DEUS

The first, 'Januaria, take thy good refreshment, and make request for us', shows how close the *refrigerium* is to the part played by the dead in making intercession for the living (p. 88, above): in the second, the situation is perfectly simple, 'May thy soul be refreshed', and in the third the idea of refreshment for the sweet soul of Antonia is found with the idea of peace.

What ultimately was implied by *refrigerium* and *pax* was life in God. SEVERA IN DEO VIVAS says an inscription from the Via Salaria Nuova.

A ring carries the single word VIVAS, 'Mayest thou live', and another carries the brief prayer, 'Lord, help'. We conclude with these, in the belief that the Christian cannot reach the life sought in the first, without the granting of the prayer offered in the second.

144 Two rings: the conclusion of the whole matter

Notes

Chapter 1

1 Eusebius *H.E.* VIII 6.7.
2 Jerome, *Ep.*, 60.12.

Chapter 2

3 *Aen.* II 755, tr. Pitt (1763).
4 Paraphrased from R. Vielliard, *Recherches sur les origines de la Rome chrétienne*, p. 20, cf. the preface, p. 7.
5 Krautheimer, *Early Christian and Byzantine Archaeology*, p. 359, cf. p. 14.
6 E. Josi, *La Venerazione degli Apostoli Pietro e Paulo*, in *Saecularia Petri et Pauli*, p. 167. (Città del Vaticano, 1969).
7 Ferrua, *Epigrammata Damasiana*, 20 (pp. 139–44, text in p. 142).
8 Paulinus, *Life of St Ambrose*, 33.
9 Duchesne, *Liber Pontificalis*, Vol. I, p. 159 (edn of 1886).
10 Meiggs, *Roman Ostia*, p. 527.
11 On Peter and Marcellinus, Ferrua, *Epigrammata Damasiana* 28, pp. 160–2, on his deprecation of burial for himself in the papal crypt, ibid. 16, pp. 119–23.
12 Krautheimer, *Early Christian, Medieval and Renaissance Art*, p. 43.
13 cf. R. Aigrain in Fliche et Martin, *Histoire de l'Eglise* V, p. 384.

Chapter 3

14 As Ferrua, *Epigrammata Damasiana*, p. 138, points out, de Rossi is not consistent about the date. He also states 1849, and 'a few months before 1850'.
15 Vasi & Nibby, *New Guide to Rome and the environs*, 3rd edn 1845.
16 Leclercq, *Manuel d'archéologie chrétienne*, I, p. 21.
17 E. tr. (1699) of Misson, *New Voyage to Italy* (1688).
18 Leclercq, in *Dictionaire d'archéologie chrétienne*, s.v. Bottari G. G.
19 Bottari, vol. III, p. 111.
20 Testini, *Le Catacombe e gli antichi Cimiteri cristiani in Rome*, p. 25.

Chapter 4

21 *Journal of Biblical Literature*, 81 (1962), p. 137.
22 Clement: *Paidagogus* 3.59.2.
23 H. J. Leon, *The Jews of ancient Rome*, pp. 259, 203.
24 Nash, *Pictorial Dictionary of Rome*, II, 359 ff.
25 Grabar, *Christian Iconography, Introduction*, p. xli.
26 Grabar, *The beginnings of Christian art* (E. tr.), p. 81 (paraphrased).

Chapter 5

27 *Revue des études juives*, 14 (1887), pp. 33 ff. and pp. 217 ff. especially pp. 242–5.
28 F. W. Beare, *The First Epistle of Peter*, pp. 148–9.
29 Philo, *De Abramo*, 46.
30 Pseudo-Cyprian, *Ad Novatianum* 5.
31 Daniélou, *Primitive Christian Symbols* (E. tr.) p. 102.
32 Wilpert, *Le Pitture delle catacombe romane*, p. 175, Pl. 83.1.
33 Theodoret, *H.E.II* 16 ff.
34 R. Garruchi, *Storia dell'arte cristiana nel primi otto secoli della Chiesa* II, Pl. 19.
35 N. Coleman in *A New Commentary on Holy Scripture*, Apocrypha, p. 121.
36 Thackeray in *A New Commentary on Holy Scripture*, Apocrypha, p. 42.
37 Thackeray, op. cit., ad. loc.
38 Garrucci II, Pl. 27.
39 Cf. A. Ferrua, *Le pitture della nuova catacomba di Via Latina*, p. 96, n. 1 and 2 on this paragraph, and in general, pp. 97–102.
40 Ferrua, op. cit., p. 103.
41 *Antike Welt* (1976), pp. 2–14.
42 Hempel, *Zeitschrift für die A. T. Wissenschaft* 73 (1961), p. 300.

Chapter 6

43 The interpretation of a much damaged picture at the Via Latina is doubtful. (Ferrua, *Le pitture . . .*, pp. 42–3), and cf. p. 84 above.
44 Wilpert, *Le Pitture . . .*, Pl. 162.2.
45 Lightfoot, *Apostolic Fathers* II, ii, p. 83.
46 Aphraates, *Hom.* I 19, ed. Parisot, p. 44.

47 A. S. Duncan-Jones, in *Liturgy and Worship*, pp. 617–18.

48 Arnold's source is A. F. Osanam, *Les poètes franciscains en Italie au treizième siècle* (Paris, 1852), which he had read not long before writing this sonnet; cf. *The poems of Matthew Arnold*, ed. Kenneth Allott (1965), p. 491.

49 Prudentius, *Cathemerinon*, 8.33–52, tr. Pope and Davis (1905).

50 E. R. Goodenough, *Journal of Biblical Literature* 81 (1962), p. 141.

Chapter 7

51 C. Cecchelli, *Monumenti cristiano-eretici di Roma*, pp. 23–4.

52 Even if one rejects the identification with Anti-Christ, it is worth while noting preoccupation with this idea both before and at this very period. Besides the references in the N.T. in I Jn 2.18, 2 Jn 7, Rev. 12.3, 13.3, 8ff., 17.7ff., cf. Matt. 24.5, 24, we have the work of Hippolytus, *On Anti-Christ*.

53 H. Chadwick, *Alexandrian Christianity*, p. 26.

54 C. Cecchelli, op. cit., p. 185.

55 C. Cecchelli, op. cit., p. 171, *una torta*.

56 C. Cecchelli, op. cit., p. 210.

57 M. Simon, *Hercule et le christianisme*, p. 173.

Chapter 8

58 *Die altchristlichen Grabstätten Siziliens.*

59 L. Bernabò Brea, *Sicily before the Greeks*, Pls 35–7, and Fig. 19 (p. 104).

60 Ruth Whitehouse, in *Antiquity* XLVI (1972), p. 278; cf. J. D. Evans, *Malta*, Pls 29–31 and pp. 129 ff.

61 G. Agnello, *La pittura paleocristiane della Sicilia* (Rome, 1952).

62 G. Agnello, op. cit., p. 23.

63 L. Bernabò Brea, *Akrae* (Catania, 1956).

64 *Verr.* 5.5.10.

65 L. Foucher, *Hadrumetum*, p. 356, n. 1452.

66 H. Achelis, *Die Catacomben von Neapel*, Pls 2–4.

67 Achelis, op. cit., p. 6.

68 Becker, *Malta Sotterranea*, Pl. XXI.

69 *Bulletin of the Valletta Museum*, I, V. for 1935.

70 T. Zammit, loc. cit., p. 193.

Chapter 9

71 Testini, op. cit., p. 196.

72 S.-L. Agnello, *Silloge di Inscrizioni paleocristiane della Sicilia* (Rome, 1953).

73 *Römische Quartalschrift* I (1887), p. 23.

74 Tertullian, *De idolatria*, 7.

75 Wilpert, *Le Pitture*, pp. 479–84, Pls 145–6.

76 cf. Testini, op. cit., pp. 205–6.

77 Delattre, *L'Epigraphia funéraire chrétienne a Carthage*, p. 79.

78 E. Josi, *Il cimitero di Callisto* (Rome, 1933), p. 104.

79 Tertullian, *Apol.* 39.

80 These three examples are taken from A.-M. Schneider, *Refrigerium* I (1928), p. 21–2.

Select Bibliography

Note: Articles in periodicals, e.g. in *Rivista di Archeologia cristiana*, or in encyclopaedias, e.g. in *Dictionnaire d'Archéologie chrétien et de Liturgie* have not usually been included, but occasionally reference to these is made in the text.

Entries with asterisks have been quoted in the text with the author's name only.

ACHELIS, H. *Die Katakomben von Neapel*, Leipzig, 1935–6.

AGNELLO, G. *La pittura paleocristiane della Sicilia*, Rome, 1952.

*AGNELLO, S.-L. *Silloge di inscrizione paleocristiane della Sicilia*, Rome, 1953.

BECKER, E. *Malta Sotterranea*, Strasbourg, 1913.

BEYER, H. W. V. & H. LEITZMANN, *Die Judische Katakombe der Villa Torlonia in Rom*, Berlin/Leipzig, 1930.

BOCK, E. & R. GOEBEL *Die Katakomben, Bilder aus der Welt des frühen Christentums*, Stuttgart, 1961.

BOLDETTI, M. A. *Osservazione sopra i cimiteri de' Santi martiri, ed antichi christiani di Roma*, Rome, 1720.

BOSIO, A. *Roma Sotterranea*, opera postuma di A. Bosio, compita disposta, ed accrescuita da G. Severani da S. Severino, Rome 1632; a later edition Rome, 1650.

BOUNNI, A. *Les catacombes d'Emese (Homs) en Syrie, Archeologia*, Nov/Dec 1970, pp. 842–8.

DU BOURGUET, P. *Le Peinture paléo-chrétienne*, Le Livre Musée, Amsterdam and Paris, 1965.

BREA, L. Bernabò *Akrae*, Catania, 1956.

CALVINO, R. La catacomba di S. Gennaro in Napoli, P.C.A.S. Napoli, 1970.

CECCHELLI, C. *Monumenti cristiano-eretici di Roma*, Rome, 1944.

DANIÉLOU, J. *Primitive Christian Symbols*, (E.tr.), London, 1964.

*DIEHL, E. *Inscriptiones Latinae Christianae veteres*, 3 vols, Berlin, 1923–31.

DUCHESNE, L. *Liber Pontificalis*, texte, introduction, et commentaire, 2 vols, Paris 1886–92.

FARIOLI, RAFFAELLA *Pitture di epoca tarda nella catacombe romane*, Ravenna, 1963.

FASOLA, U. M. *Le Catacombe de S. Gennaro a Capodimonte*, Rome, 1975.

—*The Catacomb of Domitilla and the Basilica of Saints Nereus and Achilleus*, P.C.A.S., Rome, n.d.

FERRUA, A. *Epigrammata Damasiana*, Rome, 1942.

—*Le pitture della nuova catacomba di Via Latina*. Città del Vaticano, 1960.

FOUCHER, L. *Hadrumetum*, Paris, 1964.

—Guide du Musée de Sousse, Direction des Musées nationaux de Tunisie, 1967.

—*Inventaire des Mosaïques (Sousse)*, Tunis, 1960.

*FÜHRER, J. & V. SCHULTZE *Die altchristlichen Grabstätten Siziliens*, Berlin, 1907.

GARANA, O. *Le catacombe siciliane e i loro martiri*, Palermo, 1961.

*GARRUCCI, R. *Storia della arte cristiana*, Vols I–VI, Prato, 1872–80.

GOODENOUGH, E. R. *Catacomb Art*, Journal of Biblical Literature, 81 (1962), pp. 113–42.

GOUGH, M. R. E. *The Early Christians*, London, 1961.

—*The Origins of Christian Art*, London, 1973.

GRABAR, A. N. *The Beginnings of Christian Art, 200–395*, (E.tr.) London, 1967.

—*Martyrium, recherches sur le culte des reliques et l'art chrétien antique*, 2 vols, Paris, 1946–7.

GROSSI GONDI, F. *Trattato di epigrafia cristiana, Latina e Greca, del mondo Romano occidentali*, Rome, 1920.

GUIRAUD, J. *Le commerce des reliques au commencement du IX Siècle*, Mélanges G. B. de Rossi, Rome, 1892, pp. 73–95 (Supplement aux Mélanges d'archéologie et d'histoire publiés par l'École française du Rome, Vol XII).

HERTLING, L. & E. KIRSCHBAUM *The Roman Catacombs and their Martyrs*, (E.tr.), rev. edn, London, 1960.

JOSI, E. *Il Cimitero di Callisto*, Rome, 1933. (Collezione Amici delle Catacombe).

KAUFMANN, D. *Sens et Origine des Symboles Tumulaires de l'Ancien Testament dans l'Art Chrétien primitif*, Revue des Études Juives, Vol. XIV, (1887), pp. 33–48, 217–53.

LECLERQ, H. *Manuel d'Archéologie Chrétienne*, 2 vols, Paris, 1907.

LEON, H. J. *The Jews of Ancient Rome*. Philadelphia, 1960.

LEYNAUD, A. F. *Les catacombes africaines*, 2nd edn, Alger, 1922. [A 3rd edn is in print]

MARUCCHI, ORAZIO *Le Catacombe Romane*, Rome, 1933,

MARUCCHI, H. *Éléments d'Archéologie Chrétienne*, 3 vols. 2nd French edn, Paris and Rome, 1903.

—*La Via Appia à l'époque romaine et de nos jours; Partie chrétienne* p. 273–372. Rome, 1908.

MOREY, C. R. *Early Christian Art*, Princeton, 1953.

NASH, E. *Pictorial Dictionary of Ancient Rome*, rev. edn, London, 1968.

DE ROSSI, G. B. *Roma Sotterranea*, 3 vols, Rome, 1861–77.

—*Inscriptiones Christianae Urbis Romae septimo saeculo antiquiores.* 2 vols, 1857–88, continued by A. Silvagni and A. Ferrua, Rome 1922–

SCHNEIDER, A.-M. *Refrigerium I*, Freiburg im Br., 1928.

SCHULTZE, V. *Die katakomben von San Gennaro dei Poveri in Neapel*, Jena, 1877.

STYGER, P. *Die Römischen Katakomben*, Berlin, 1933.

—*Römische martyrergrüfte*, 2 vols, Berlin, 1935.

TESTINI, P. *Archeologia cristiana*, Rome, 1958.

—*Le catacombe e gli antichi cimiteri cristiani in Roma*, Bologna, 1966.

—*The Christian Catacombs in Rome*, Ente provinciale per il turismo di Roma, n.d.

TOYNBEE, J. M. C. *Death and Burial in the Roman World*, London, 1971.

WEIDEL, W. [VEIDLE, V.] *The Baptism of Art. The Religion of the Catacomb Paintings*, London, 1950.

*WILPERT, G. *Le Pitture delle Catacombe romane*, 2 vols, Rome, 1903.

—*Die Katakombengemälde und ihre alten Copien*, Freiburg im Br., 1891.

ZAMMIT, C. G. *The Tal Bistra Catacombs*, Bulletin of the Museum, Valletta, Malta, Vol. I, No. 5, February 1935, pp. 165–87.

ZAMMIT, Sir T. *An Early Christian Rock-Tomb, on the Hal Resqun Bridle Road at Gudia*, Reference under previous entry, pp. 189–95.

List of Illustrations